FORKAPPLEPRESS.ORG/
THE-CORE-REVIEW/ISSUE1

Scan this QR code for full online access to this issue of *The Core Review*, and to view visual narrative submissions in color.

FORKAPPLEPRESS.ORG
@FORKAPPLEPRESS

The Core Review is a biannual literary journal. We accept submissions January through March and July through September on Submittable. Visit our website for detailed submission guidelines: forkapplepress.org/core

The Core Review is an imprint of Fork Apple Press, a small independent literary press publishing work that expands beyond a core, essentialized "truth" to challenge a monolithic point of view. Fork Apple Press: 390 Broadway, Somerville, MA 02145. Telephone: +1 (857) 242-1260. Web address: forkapplepress.org. Email: forkapplepress@gmail.com.

ISBN: 9798330571987
Printed and distributed by IngramSpark
Cover design by Nico Léger

The opinions expressed in this journal are solely those of the authors. All rights revert to the authors upon publication.

© 2024 by Fork Apple Press LLC

Contents

POETRY

JANE FEINSOD	6	Dinner Party in Green
KARAGIN RUFF	12	If Jesus and Judas walked into a bar after the last supper
	70	Said the Lily Leaf to the Slug
ZACH SEMEL	14	*Top Chef* S13 E8: On Microgreens
KAMI WESTHOFF	20	Last Gasp
AUTUMN H. THOMAS	44	Dermatillomania
GRAEME GUTTMANN	46	Dead Deer, Nebraska
	47	Going home the weekend the boy I used to love died
L. WARD ABEL	78	A Color of Wheat to the Forest Wall
MACK ROGERS	80	if you had truly tasted the rainbow, you would know it tastes like the drive to Great Smoky Mountains National Park in the fall

PROSE

SOFIA GRADY	8	Inheritance
CHAR GARDNER	18	Market Day
E.E. KING	21	Oldest Man in the Skateboard Park

HEIDI KLAASSEN	23	Matchbook Dominoes
JASMINE BASUEL	42	Dinner with Enya
ANTHONY CORREALE	52	The Imaginers
AMELIA K.	71	One of These Things First
WESTON CUTTER	72	Of Course You Can't Really Change Anyone
ARI KETZAL	82	Coupon Royals

VISUAL NARRATIVE

JAMES GOUDIE	38	On Identity
CHLOE TATE	50	Can't Go Home

CONTRIBUTORS   89

Masthead

Poetry Editor
KATIE MIHALEK

Prose Editor
VIVIAN WALMAN-RANDALL

Creative Director
NICO LÉGER

Copy Chief
CAMERON SCHOETTLE

The Core Review

Fall 2024 • Issue 1

Dinner Party In Green

JANE FEINSOD

thank you for saving my place
at the table while I was stuck
picking out gray from under
my nails can I ask you and
I mean this politely can I ask
what's on the menu tonight
I know
that ladies take off their corsets
when they eat they go bare breasted
is it true I'm sorry to ask this is it
true about the aftertaste
I heard
something that it has notes of
green chartreuse and alchemy
it stings the gums like hell but
is otherwise pleasant and
oh goodness
I didn't notice you
were dissolving I didn't see
your feet under the table
melting in your brogues
staining the carpet emerald
I get it
I do it too sometimes try not to get
sick if it happens well then try
not to vomit if you do vomit try

to keep it in your mouth if it gets
out you'll make such a scene and
oh that's the worst part
the worst feeling
I know

Inheritance

SOFIA GRADY

In my earliest memory, I am curled into my mother's lap on an overnight flight, we are draped in a flimsy JetBlue blanket, and she is drinking tomato juice. I grew up in California, though my mother is from New York, so many of our holidays were spent in transit. Twice a year, we would pack our favorite things into a brimming suitcase and board a red-eye to her family home. On every flight we took, my mother ordered tomato juice.

In the summers, when the humidity threatened to smother you if you breathed too deeply, we spent our time in New York learning to fish in the lake behind my uncle's house and flinging ourselves from the railings of the back porch into the above-ground pool below. In the winters, when the wind gnawed your cheeks pink and snow snuck into the waistband of your pants, we spent our time in the kitchen.

My grandmother was an amazing cook. A robust, Italian woman with a dark shadow over her upper lip and perfectly permed hair, she layered lasagna in blankets of ricotta cheese, dipped broccoli in hollandaise sauce, finished alfredo with egg yolk and heavy cream, and wrapped cheese-stuffed hot dogs in bacon. "I'm making the gravy!" she'd holler into the living room, letting the beloved family spaghetti sauce splatter onto her apron.

The sauce recipe, a matriarchal rite of passage in my family, is my great-grandmother Mary's. At seventeen, she married great-grandfather Frank, whose first wife died during an underground abortion, leaving him with four children and a house to tend to. Mary and Frank grew up in the same neighborhood—she swore that she loved him since she was five. During their first dance as husband and wife, Frank whispered to Mary that he would never love her, he just needed a mother to his children.

For years, she did just that. She raised his children, cooked his meals, and tended to his home while Frank had rampant affairs and beat her until her eyes were blue and she lost her hearing in her left ear. When she became pregnant, Frank told her he did not want her bearing his children and brought home herbs for her to abort it. That night, once Frank fell asleep, my great-grandmother went into the kitchen, grabbed the same knife she had used to cook supper that night, climbed onto his snore-heaving chest, pressed the sharpest edge of the knife to his throat and whispered, "If you ever lay a hand on me again, I will kill you in your sleep." The following summer, Mary gave birth to her only child, Margaret Francis.

The secret to our sauce recipe is simple. A spoonful of sugar, to cut the acidity, and a single bay leaf for flavor, which if ingested in full can be deadly.

My grandmother's kitchen was the center of the house. On one side it connected to the foyer and the stairwell. On the other, the living room and the patio, and behind a door parallel to the fridge, the stairs to my grandfather's basement and workshop. So, if you wanted to get anywhere in the house, you had to walk past my grandmother and through her kitchen. When I was young, my grandmother would sit me on the counter, and place black olives on the tips of each of my fingers so I would not eat the cheese out of the bowl as she grated it. From here, I could watch the smoke plume off the end of my grandfather's cigarette on the couch, see the old western on the television, and wave to my mother at the dining room table. My grandmother's kitchen was perpetually damp—the Formica cabinets, dented from a sailing pair of pliers, waned with moisture and the drawers crackled when her hip knocked them shut. My mother's hairline is adorned with a scar from slipping after coming in from the snow and opening her head on the island's edge. There's a faint stain on the floor beneath the sink that my grandmother always pulls the mat over when it strays from its place.

On November 22, 1963, while cooking dinner and listening to the news that John F. Kennedy had been assassinated, my grandmother, nearly five months pregnant, started to have terrible pain in her lower back and abdomen. Unable to make it up the stairs, my grandfather brought over a bucket and placed it right on the kitchen floor. She quickly began gushing blood and crying. Unsure what was happening, she became hysterical. In an attempt to soothe her, my grandfather started to sift through the blood that had splashed into the bucket. Eventually, he found a clump the size of his palm. It would have been a boy. Two springs later, my grandmother gave birth to her only daughter, Theresa Mary.

My mother was wild growing up. She fell in love with Jeff in the seventh grade, but it wasn't until their junior year of high school that he considered paying her any attention. From then on, Jeff was my mother's partner in chaos. After losing her virginity to Jeff, my mother found out she was pregnant. She was certain she couldn't be, because they had only done it "halfway" so she must still be a virgin, though Jeff didn't pull out because there was a new comforter on my mother's bed, and they didn't want to make a mess. After asking Lisa, her most reliable friend, for money, Jeff drove my mother to have an abortion. When she came to after the procedure, the doctor was sitting with her, holding her hand. He was an Indian man with a soft face and said she had been screaming in her sleep. By the time Jeff picked her up, she was hysterical.

My mother and I do not travel together anymore; though my holidays are still spent in transit—traveling home to California from the opposite coast, curled into my solo window seat. During my time home, my mother and I share her bathroom mirror for our morning routine. We take turns sipping coffee from our cups, she tells me I am wearing too much blush, and I smudge her eyeshadow into place with the corner of my thumb. We feel close. I begin to miss her even while she is standing beside me.

I moved to Washington D.C. to finish my bachelor's degree in the summer of 2018. The following October in my college dorm room, I woke to the sound of my own weeping. I remember being wet. The same thick wetness covered my sheets—I was bleeding. I made it to the bathroom floor before losing consciousness.

When I opened my eyes again, I was in an unfamiliar white room, dressed in an oversized paper gown that chafed at my skin and a hospital bracelet with gray lettering, *Sofia Margaret*. When the nurse finally came in through the drawstring curtain, she brought me a carton of tomato juice with a green straw. She called me "sweetie" and told me that I hemorrhaged during a miscarriage. I didn't know that I was pregnant.

The following Christmas in California, my mother curled my grown-up body into her lap and stroked my hair while I cried. She told me that once, decades ago, she'd written a letter to the little one that could have been.

I imagined *it* would have been a *she*—sage eyes muddled with the deep brown of her Italian roots, a prominent nose and two dark eyebrows that threatened to join like her mother's. So, I wrote to her.

I would have liked to be your mother. I think I might have made a good mother. But I'm glad you don't have to hear your father and I yell over your Barney tapes at bedtime. I would have dug up those Barney tapes if you'd come. My father would have bought us a yellow cassette player that I'd place on the nightstand beside your changing table—close enough for you to hear over the whirring of your mobile, but not so close that the clicking of its end woke you, like it did me when I was little.

I was a child when you were supposed to come. I wonder now if I would have made it work if you had. I'm afraid I wouldn't have.

I wonder if you'll come back to me someday, in a body that is ready to survive with me, when my body is ready to care for you.

I hope so.

If Jesus and Judas walked into a bar after the last supper

KARAGIN RUFF

There's a bar in Jerusalem with a
door agape as the mouth of Satan, where
Jesus and Judas sit thigh to thigh. One
orders bourbon, and one orders wine. A
jukebox hymn plays in their covet silence.
With upturned palms, Jesus sweats the question;
how does one begin to resurrect what
hasn't died? Judas cups Jesus's worried
hands, "Whatever it is, we'll be alright."
The headlights through the window crown Jesus
in a jagged branching light. He is the
future king of killing darlings, this is
his coronation night. "I need you to
betray me?" Jesus begs, his lips stained by
grape blood. Judas asks, "Why?" Jesus chokes the
answer, "If your hand stumbles, cut it off.
If your lips tremble kiss to condemn." His
eyes make a cross of the table, carving
out Judas's embrace. "No apple tastes as
good as your lips. Heaven's truths hold nothing
to your lies, but I was a son before
I was a man, and you're what stands between
me and God, so I'm asking you to step
aside." Judas downs his glass, tasting the

bitter honey goodbye. "And would we meet
again in the place where the sun only
rises?" Jesus doesn't lift his head. "You'll
be prince of a different kingdom, but
I'll build us a bridge. We'll sit side by side.
We'll throw our crowns atop the frozen lake...."
As Jesus marched on, Judas wished they could
be nailed to the night as new stars or a
neon bar sign, their souls dancing in the
same fires. His carpenter companion had
built his hopes too high. No construction could
mend a religion. Still Judas smiled, "If
we'll be closer in hell than we could be
in heaven I'll suffer any torment."
Only the glasses wept on the table
when the men lynched their bodies from the booth.
At dawn, Judas gave zealots their fable.
One kiss which condemns two. As Lucifer's
new cavity, Judas raises a glass
in the monster's teeth, "Here's to a happy hell."

Top Chef S13 E8: On Microgreens

ZACH SEMEL

1

"Where's the beef?" someone says. Tom Colicchio holds up a tiny radish and shakes his head, "Dainty, dainty," the plant almost breaking between his fingers. It's muscly proteins that he wants: food that can withstand being torn apart with bare hands, gnashed between teeth with what care he decides it deserves.

2

Morning affirmation: men don't see
        you and notice every flaw
as often as you think, no
        evaluative eyes peeking
into shower stalls; don't worry, men
        don't take you in
for longer than a glance.

3

Dish concept: using proprietary technology,
        the taste of my finger
                in a man's mouth
            without them ever needing to come

close to my bony wrists.

4

My partner's ex would only eat
        cheeseburgers and who wouldn't
want that
        in another person: to be
welcomed like
        American cheese oozing
between fingers, sweet
        taste of iron making teeth ring.

5

Sometimes I think I smell
        the problem
trapped in the back

of my fridge: that I could never prepare
        myself carefully enough to share
this body, spoon myself
        between lips, be a broth

dripping from chins.
        I lie in bed and wonder:
are these legs like roots
        growing out of bedsheets, dirt
crumbs clinging to hairs, every inch
        a tangled mess of cells?

6

>   On *No Reservations*, there was a chef
>   who tried his own tasting menu every month
>   because if you don't love what you make
>   how could anyone else?

7

Google suggests that I take a look
at Padma Lakshmi's scar; all at once I remember
how curious we can be, how inquisitive
fingers may seek out imperfections
to be close to, arrows on the body
gesturing towards the parts that want
to be found.

8

Dish concept: my skin shivering
against a metal plate, family-style
flesh for four-to-six, full table
of hands fighting for mouthful after mouthful,
call my stretch marks *marbling*.

9

Recipe:
1. Pancakes in the morning (after)
2. a man who knows to put wet in after dry
3. warm butter falling into flour
4. oil licks off fingers
5. eggs, sugar, salt

6. him flipping pancakes
7. skillful wrist
8. his fingers wrapped around the panhandle tight
9. like his palm could swallow it all in one gulp

10

Morning affirmation: you look like the sun gave you attention
while you sat in soil, like if you were served
raw, all the wispy fibers (your loose, shaking parts)
would send light back out: chlorophyll flares
singeing diners' hair. It's sunny and clear, but I still see you
from a mile away. Even if your neon glow
was just a road-stop sign, I'd want to pull over and eat.

Market Day

CHAR GARDNER

"Only the poor shop at City Market," says Gabija, as I rave about the fresh garlic I bought last week. She prefers Maxima, the new supermarket. Eastern Europe's headlong rush to mass consumerism depresses me. Six years ago, when I began working in Vilnius, a few Soviet-style shops could still be found. No one was sorry to see them go. To the new generation, Maxima is heaven: a clean, well-lit, pristine palace of self-service, spread out over vast aisles of neatly stacked goods. Abundant displays of junk food, shrimp from Bangladesh, unlimited toilet paper, cosmetics, and imported alcohol. Cakes, leaden with sugary frosting! Wheeling massive carts through the thoroughly modern emporium is a weekend outing for entire families.

Underpaid Russian women, left behind when Communism collapsed, command the checkout counters, where they visit the fury of their demoted social status on the newly prosperous Lithuanians buying Marlboros and meat.

As church bells ring out over the city, I count my cash, grab my backpack, and set out on foot for City Market. On Sunday mornings the sidewalk along Bokšto Street is often tracked with Saturday night blood.

Opposite my apartment, a high stone wall (remnant of the city's medieval past) is a gathering place for the young. Boys in fake leather jackets and pointy-toed white loafers and girls in stilettos and impossibly tight jeans make their way on cobbled streets, lugging supersized plastic bottles of cheap beer. Pockets bulge with flasks of local vodka. They hoist each other up onto the wall and settle like birds, singing drunkenly long into the night. Toward morning, fights break out.

But, today, only shards of broken glass and crumpled cigarette packs litter the sidewalk.

The cavernous yellow-brick market resembles a nineteenth-century train station. Inside, a clutch of aggressive women hawk used plastic bags for one Lita each. I point to my backpack and move on. From thirty feet up, sunbeams stream through hundreds of dirty windowpanes into an arena echoing with sounds of commerce conducted in an archaic tonal language. Smells of sauerkraut, warm bread, and the B.O. of secondhand clothing and footwear.

Bent-backed ladies all in black touch and sniff every apple and cabbage, inspect each egg, and haggle over prices. Ragged children swarm the honey sellers for a free taste smeared on strips of paper. A half-naked teenager ducks down between clothing racks to try on a bra, and an overly tanned blonde in a tank top, cigarette pack tucked into her cleavage, waits in line for a bag of chicken feet.

The Lithuanian language, neither Slavic nor Germanic, and nearly eradicated by the Soviets, is hellish to pronounce. I can say *ačiū* (like a sneeze) which means *thank you*. The letter *S*, with a bird on top, is pronounced *sh*. *Šitas* means *this*. I approach the chicken lady, the bacon man, and the mushroom girl with her glorious golden chanterelles. I point and say, *Šitas, ačiū*, and they slowly pick through my hand full of coins for payment.

Finally, my backpack sags with carrots, cucumbers, potatoes, honey, and fresh bread, and I head out to confront the end of market day. In a row along the curb stand the misbegotten aged. Jobless and bereft without the Soviet bureaucracy, they offer for sale small bouquets of wildflowers tied with bits of curled birthday ribbon, a package of pantyhose, loose tea bags, a can of motor oil. *Prašau, Prašau*, they murmur. Please.

Last Gasp

KAMI WESTHOFF

At sunset, your fist reverses into palm,
reveals the perfect skipping rock.
While March's last gasp slaughters the sky,
you show our daughter the hip-crick,
the crater of pointer and thumb, the wrist
flick that galaxies the sea. You've done so little
of this lately, I tuck my complaints into a chasm
of later, watch the surface absorb each wound,
each ring expanding into an orbit of okay.
While she practices, I scoot so there's room
for you on the log. You sit, then flick a spider
before its legs find mine. It's easy, this kind of us.
Down shore, a heron hunts, patient as a century.
Above shore, seagulls giggle and gawk at our daughter
who is so terrible at skipping rocks that when she draws
back her arm, we duck in every direction.

The Oldest Man in the Skateboard Park

E.E. KING

Although Cameron Inc was almost fifty, he loved to board in the skateboard park.

What was this old white-haired man doing? the teenagers wondered. Bonking and carving as if he was one of them, as if he was young, as if he had a future ahead of him instead of only a past behind.

At seventeen, he'd been a king. The most skillful boy in the park, but all who'd admired his skill, and measured themselves against him were gone, most to banks, boardrooms, law firms, or tech companies. Many already retired, some not just from boarding but from life.

It wasn't so much that Cameron had lost his adolescence, as that it had slipped away unnoticed. He still felt young, if being unchanged is young. His mind and heart no more developed than when he was seventeen.

But his heart, though metaphorically untouched, had physically altered. It had hardened and grown fatty. Thumping unevenly like a landed fish as he flawlessly executed his signature move, a backside, mongo-foot nollie. It leaped, giving a final gasp as he landed hard on his side right across the quarter pipe ramp.

The skateboard park regulars who usually ignored him, viewing him as an embarrassment, a warning of things to come, ebbed around him, forming an uneven circle. They watched as he wheezed and shivered—a beached whale, a hardening dinosaur. After a few minutes he lay still.

The boys waited, till Sid, always the boldest, sped down the quarter pipe ramp, spun a full cab over Cameron's fallen body seamlessly landing on an edge, ending with a shove-it that crushed Cameron's ankle bones with a grinding snap.

The boys gasped in admiration. It was so difficult to spin on soft surfaces. They lined up waiting to try their skill.

For a second time, Cameron was a part of the park. No longer a king, but a ramp. Yet once again providing a pinnacle to scale, a barometer against which young boys could measure their skill.

Matchbook Dominoes

HEIDI KLAASSEN

In the summer after I graduated high school, I had a job working for a lawyer. He was the executor of a deceased man's estate, and he needed someone to clear out his client's house so it could be sold. My friend D's dad knew the lawyer and recommended the two of us for the job. He offered up his old, brown Ford Ranchero as a work vehicle to haul stuff to the dump. We were told the job could take a month or more—the house was pretty messy. We wouldn't be expected to actually clean the house—that would come after we left, when all the man's possessions had been dealt with. Still, I don't think any synonym for "messy" could have prepared us for what we discovered on the first day.

There are theories around the psychology of hoarding based on human needs like control and comfort. People hoard things because they are creating a safe space for themselves, or they're replacing a lack of love with objects, or they genuinely believe the items they keep will eventually be needed. I have kept things for all these reasons. When we assign value or emotion to something, it becomes difficult to part with it. What we keep and what we discard says so much about us.

Stockpiling looks a bit like hoarding. It involves deliberately holding onto resources that could become scarce due to unforeseen events, like when people hoarded toilet paper during the pandemic. Some items, like Québec maple syrup, are deliberately stockpiled to control the price. If this is done on the stock market, it's called cornering the market, and it's illegal. But with maple syrup it's okay. It's Canada, so it could not possibly be nefarious. In the US, there's a National Strategic Stockpile of pharmaceuticals and other necessities in hidden locations around the country. It has been deployed during events like 9/11 and Hurricane

Katrina. In Norway, the Svalbard Global Seed Vault has a collection of plant life should the world need to be re-grown. In the UK, the CryoArks Biobank is developing the first comprehensive zoological collection in case we need to repopulate the earth with animals after they have all been decimated by human idiocy.

We showed up at the dead man's house in jeans and T-shirts with rubber gloves, as instructed. The lawyer met us at the front and pushed open the door to the small bungalow, where we were stopped almost immediately by stacks of…stuff. Piles of newspapers were like pillars around the living room. A mound of bread bag ties the size of a bulldog blocked the entrance to the kitchen. There were unopened Christmas presents and stacks of mail dating back years. The smell in the house was pungent, like the windows had never been opened. The three of us climbed over hills of shopping bags and magazines, making our way into the house. I moved toward a closed bedroom door and the lawyer stopped me.

"My client took care of his mother in her final years. That was her room. I don't think he went in there at all after she passed away," he warned.

I nodded and turned the doorknob. There was resistance behind the door from the mess inside the room. D was behind me, and we recoiled, wincing from the smell. The bare mattress was deeply stained. The smell of urine was intense. We closed the door.

"As I mentioned, you won't have to clean anything, but you may want to get that mattress to the dump first thing," said the lawyer.

A friend of mine passed away suddenly. He was not my best friend, not even a close friend—not that I didn't see him worthy of being a close friend. We'd shared some good times—a mutual friend's wedding, some parties and TV industry golf tournaments. We had worked together, on occasion, and decidedly not worked together—a day of laughter that involved smoking up during errands for a talk show we worked on. I'd last seen him at his eldest son's funeral, after a brain aneurysm took a gifted boy with his dad's infectious smile. In the days following the tragedy, I had consumed every social media post his dad put out to the world, declaring his son a superhero for the donated organs that saved six lives. His unimaginable loss was a miraculous gift for six families. This man had lost his fourteen-year-old child in an everyday moment, life robbed from him in an instant. Somehow, he had managed to find the positive, to see light in the darkest of times.

Now, he was suddenly gone, taken by a stroke on a regular day at work. His family, no doubt incredulous at the cruelty of this, fulfilled his wishes to donate his organs and again strangers were gifted with life from a tragic loss.

I think about him a lot, wondering about an afterlife, a reunion with his son. I have doubts about this outcome, but it's soothing to believe it. I wonder about the parts of him that have changed lives, that live on—like his son's body—in a stranger who needed someone to die so they could live. I think about those videos on Instagram, like the one where the bride is walked down the aisle by the man who received her dead father's heart, or the clip of the grieving father, an older white man listening by stethoscope to the sound of his daughter's beating heart inside a young black man. They cry together, overcome by the horrific tragedy that enabled something so beautiful.

Over the next few weeks, D and I made many trips to the dump. We put aside anything of value for an estate sale and everything else was bagged and thrown into the back of the Ranchero. I brought my camera and took black-and-white photos to document our weird summer job, snapping shots of D at the dump or sitting on the front stoop, taking a break from the smell and the heat. We discovered vast collections of objects—stacks of takeout containers, an assortment of odd forks, and hundreds of matchbooks.

There was an element of macabre gloom about sorting through a stranger's possessions after their death. We were eighteen and invincible, but the idea that what we leave behind could be examined and judged by strangers still felt a little awful. Always interested in a good story, I tried to piece together the life of this man. I knew only that he had been a successful oil and gas executive. It was obvious there were people who had cared about him, at least enough to deliver Christmas gifts, even if he never opened them. There were also large supplies of food items, like someone had gone to Costco for bottled water and juice, bulk supplies of toilet paper and boxes of packaged snacks that remained unopened, piled up in the living room.

Over the course of the pandemic, the world's billionaires added over a trillion dollars to their holdings while small businesses closed, unemployment soared, and food shortages drove up the basic costs of survival. While politicians and public health experts floundered with inconsistently applied rules, the top 0.1% of households sat atop their $12 trillion and looked down on the rest of us. This unprecedented world health crisis made a lot of the world's richest people much richer, and their perceived philanthropy provided convenient tax deductions for their growing fortunes.

It's not just billionaires who hoard wealth. Even the moderately wealthy are okay with watching the world burn from their spacious summer cottages. The super-rich could solve world hunger and poverty with one trip to the ATM, but they choose not to. Hoarding wealth assures the continuation of the wealth. There are no rich without poor, so it is in their best interests to keep a large segment of the population hungry enough to work in their dangerous factories, their shitty fast-food restaurants and cancer-causing mines.

Defenders of the ultra-rich say the uber-wealthy create jobs when they do spend, that their need for real estate, yachts and luxury hotels puts paychecks in pockets. They say the money that billionaires are hoarding supplies banks with capital for small business loans and mortgages for ordinary folks who need to borrow half a million dollars to provide their families with a place to sleep at night.

Chuck Collins gave away his Oscar Mayer family inheritance to work at making the world a better place. He tries to convince the ridiculously wealthy to do good things with their money, showing them that philanthropy for causes like saving the environment can be in their own best interests too. He distinguishes those with $30 million or more as the "oligarch class," people who have more money than they require to meet their needs, moneyed folk who now focus on using their riches to gain power and grow their wealth. They're the ones golfing with Donald Trump and Vladimir Putin, people who wouldn't think twice about stepping on impoverished children to get into their private jets.

It was difficult to move through the house. There was so much stuff, we spent the first day clearing a path through the living room, into the kitchen and through to the back door. To open all the windows, we had to clear the way to those also. As much as it was an inconvenience, we both agreed on day one that we would not, or rather could not, use the bathroom in the house. We opted instead to make the short drive to D's house when one or both of us had to go. We cleared out whatever was stashed around the tub and toilet and shut the door, leaving years of filth for the cleaning company that would arrive after we were long gone.

It was over a week before we ventured downstairs. The basement was as expected—gloomy, damp, and unfinished, with concrete floors and mildew-stained walls. It smelled, but it was different from the pungent, closed-in human smells of the main floor. Where the upstairs felt almost too lived-in, the basement seemed like no one had been down there in years. D took his boom box down there and started in on the endless accumulation while he blasted N.W.A., Anthrax, and Public Enemy. It was in this basement that D coined a term I still use today: dust buffalos (since "bunnies" was clearly inadequate).

Whenever one of us discovered something interesting in the house, we'd call to the other and commiserate over the potential value of the item, or perhaps just the weirdness of it. One day, I heard D calling my name from the basement.

"I found something!"

"Is it good?" I yelled back.

"For some people, I guess?"

I ran downstairs to where D sat on the floor in front of a cardboard box. He pointed at it, saying nothing. Inside were dozens of porn magazines from the seventies and eighties, specifically gay male porn. The colour was a little faded, but the magazines were still in fairly good shape.

"What should we do with it?" I asked. D shrugged.

I was eighteen and it was the before-times, pre-internet. I'd never seen gay porn, so I had to check it out. I pulled the top magazine off the stack. On the cover was a handsome man with dark hair and a handlebar mustache. I flipped through a few pages and quickly returned the magazine to the box. I felt like I'd just learned someone's well-kept secrets.

Pop-up repair events and local fixing collectives are becoming more prevalent, given the unreasonable cost of living. They're happening as an effort to save money, but also to save the landfill from wasted items that are fixable. Most people don't want to spend the time repairing their belongings. It's easier to toss that toaster in the garbage and buy a cheap new one on Amazon. There's too much stuff in the world—too much choice and too many old things languishing at the dump. In the UK, one group of repair volunteers carry a box of miscellaneous items called the "Lonely Parts Club." The fact we need a group of people to organize and volunteer their time to fix our broken stuff says so much about humans. Why are we being taught trigonometry in school, but no one knows how to mend a sweater? A population that knows how to square dance or name the major players in the Boer War seems useless if we can't repair a lamp or restore a scuffed tabletop. The global pandemic brought so many issues to light, and one of them was exactly this—a dependence on more, new, too much. Shouldn't the lockdowns have taught us the need to develop a skillset of resourcefulness instead of producing a soft middle class who knows how to bake the occasional loaf of artisan bread?

We paced the basement, glancing at the box of porn. On the one hand, it was a box of old magazines, possibly worthless. On the other, they were well-preserved, vintage publications, and could be of some value to the estate. I knew a little about this man, through my dad, who also worked in the oil and gas industry. There had never been any mention of the man's sexuality, only that he'd long been single and taken care of his elderly mother. The contents of this box likely would have come as a surprise to everyone who knew this man professionally.

In the end, we decided to put the box into the back of the Ranchero and take it to the dump. Leaving it to be sold or donated could have outed the owner of the house, and this seemed like something he'd gone to great lengths to conceal. He'd been a man of the Silent Generation, and he'd chosen to keep this part of his life quiet.

When I first moved out on my own, at eighteen, I wanted a pet and wasn't permitted to keep a dog in my crappy apartment, so I adopted a cat from the Humane Society. It was post-Halloween in 1993, and River Phoenix had just died on the sidewalk outside the Viper Room in Los Angeles. I named my black cat Phoenix and brought her home to my new digs. She clawed my second-hand sofa. She scratched the cigarette-burned carpet. She climbed everything with her claws, including my leg and the half-dead Christmas tree I dragged home in December. I made the decision to have her declawed. I was lonely and wanted a cuddly companion, and my hands and arms were constantly getting carved up by her tiny razors.

Over the next few years, I moved three more times, ending up in my cherished fourth-floor studio in The Lorraine Apartments. On a warm September evening, all of my windows were open as I folded laundry and watched *Friends* on my ancient, eighty-pound TV. Phoenix was sitting on the window ledge a few feet away. It was the episode where Chandler hides all of Joey's underwear, forcing him to go commando in a rented tuxedo. As revenge, Joey pledges to do the opposite, so he puts on all of Chandler's clothes and starts lunging in them, still commando. I laughed at Matt LeBlanc and glanced at the window. Phoenix was gone. Cats are known to be stealthy, so I assumed she'd silently jumped to the floor and run off to hide. Still, something didn't feel right. I looked in all of her usual hiding places—under the couch, deep inside my messy closet, but I couldn't locate her. I employed the failsafe last resort, opening a can of tuna. Only my other cat, Nelson, came running. There was only one explanation, and it seemed impossible: Phoenix had fallen out of the window.

I grabbed a flashlight and ran downstairs to the parking lot. Phoenix was silent, hiding under a parked car. When I pulled her out, I discovered one of her front legs was badly broken.

The vet told me her leg was likely unfixable. She gave me three choices: I could risk surgery, which may not work and started at $1,500; I could have her leg amputated for $800; or I could have her euthanized for $75. I asked what most people did in situations like this. I was flat broke, but I was willing to do almost anything to save Phoenix. She said most people had the pet put down, that they didn't like the aesthetic of a three-legged animal. I was horrified—people would rather lose their pets than get them back slightly altered? She said this trend was about the appearance but also the mistaken belief that a dog or cat couldn't have a full, active life with only three limbs. Owners who did choose amputation usually decided to keep the shoulder because it looked better. I asked what purpose that would serve for Phoenix. The answer was none—it would be a shoulder joint moving as though the leg was still attached, but it would be more symmetrical, and that's what most pet owners preferred. I decided to go ahead with the amputation, shoulder and all. I would beg and borrow my way to saving my cat.

Phoenix lived to be seventeen years old. When she passed away, I found her on the carpet of the home I shared with my growing family. She looked as though she'd been leaping through the air, having died mid-jump. She'd moved homes with me five more times and learned to catch flies out of mid-air with her one, declawed front paw. I never forgave myself for having her claws removed. At the time, it had seemed like a necessity, to preserve my damage deposits and my stuff. I believe Phoenix may not have fallen four stories if she'd had claws to dig into the wooden window ledge. I hope I made the right choice for her with the amputation, to leave behind what she could no longer use.

Some days, we sat on the front stoop, dreading the dingy, poorly-lit rooms with clutter blocking the windows. We breathed in the last moments of fresh air before crossing the threshold into that place, where it felt hard to breathe, where the smell took over and clung to our clothes and hair like cigarette smoke. Being in that house made us lose our appetites, and most days we skipped lunch. It was hard to summon hunger in a building where everything had been left to rot. We ate at home, after showers, after distance from discovering the fallout of human neglect.

Human organs have become a commodity traded both legally and illegally. The World Health Organization says one in ten organ transplants is a trafficked human organ. In some countries, there's "transplant tourism," where you can get an all-inclusive package that features a new kidney installed while you're visiting. It's perfectly legal. Most of the time the organs come from people in poor countries and the recipients are from rich ones. A guy in Bangladesh will sell a kidney to feed his family and then end up sick and unable to work. Meanwhile, some white dude is back on the golf course, filtering craft beer through his thrifted kidney.

We were getting paid by the hour, so we tried to stretch the job out as much as possible. We were also trying to add some levity to a weird and gross situation. When we took a break, we'd step out into the unkept yard, breathing in the fresh air. Getting outside helped to ease my low-grade germaphobia. The property had been neglected for a long time, and thousands of ants crawled in and around the dry root system of the pine tree in front of the house. They were everywhere, climbing up our legs if we stood still for too long. It started as a defence tactic. D took a sip of water and sprayed it from his mouth, aiming for the ants. Soon, we were keeping track of how many ants we could bomb with our spit. We invented rules for the game, like having to fire from a seated position on the front steps or getting bonus points for soaking more than one ant in one shot. The concrete path to the front door became dotted in lighter grey, our mouth-water having cleaned tiny patches of the filthy sidewalk.

When I turned twenty-one, my mom gave me a photo album she'd created. It's a large book with a glossy red cover. She wanted to document the first twenty-one years of my life, as a keepsake. I cherish this album, and I love that she pored over the photographs, likely thinking about each memory as she chose them for the album. As a mom now, I can imagine the mixed emotions of assembling something like this. But there was always something about the album that was missing. I flipped through the stiff pages again and again, looking through the photos of me at different stages of growth. Then it hit me: in most of the photos, it's just me. The surrounding scene has been cut away, likely my mom's sweet way of putting the focus on me—but the result is a collection of photographs without context. Now that I'm over twice the age of that album, it's strange to look back at a collection of images from my childhood without the background to give me clues about the memories contained within them. Without these visual cues, it's just me, looking younger and then older. There's no story.

When we grew tired of spit-bombing the ants, we moved on to the backyard with a garbage bag full of matchbooks. We painstakingly laid them out so that each one was opened and connected to the next. We created a spiraling pattern, curving and twisting the matchbooks down the concrete path all the way to the small garage in the backyard. When we were satisfied with our design, we lit the first cluster of matches and waited.

There were a couple of burnouts—matchbooks that weren't close enough together to catch the flame—but after two or three false starts, the inferno of dominoes lit up. Each one flared and sparked, then died down as the carboard cover burned into the next book. Once burned out, they left a charred mark on the sidewalk in the pattern we'd made. When D's dad stopped by later that afternoon to see how we were doing, he stood staring at the spiral of char on the concrete, scratching his head.

I wondered why these objects had been saved, for what purpose? Maybe there was no reason, other than just having them. Why the bread bag ties? Hundreds of them, what must have been years of saving. What would this man have thought about us clearing out his hoard—would he be relieved? Horrified? It seemed, despite his prestigious career, he had few objects of any monetary value. His house and yard looked as though they hadn't been maintained at all. What he did have were thousands of relatively useless objects, like piles of nametags from conferences he'd attended over his well-publicized career.

I've always had a problem getting rid of fabric. I enjoy sewing because, like writing, it's an act of creating something from nothing. Pieces are cut and attached by thread through a machine needle or one in my hand, and the result is a piece of art or a utilitarian object, or both.

Much of my fabric hoarding has come from the idea behind my practice as a fibre artist. I make bags using the discarded fabrics from the interior design industry, repurposed materials like old leather jackets, and the beautiful vintage fabrics unearthed from basements when people downsize. I like the idea that my bags are made almost entirely from materials that would have gone to the landfill.

As a child, I loved interior design sample books, flipping through the fabric pages and running my fingers over the twills and velvets and shiny brocades. I marvelled at the fact these books had no real value because the samples were too small to be useful. As an adult, I began collecting them—collecting being the less alarming version of hoarding. These small pieces of luxury were garbage to everyone else, outdated décor samples tossed in the trash. For me, they were pieces of one-of-a-kind handbags I made from something formerly useless.

In parts of China, the fabrics used to create a new baby's clothing are sourced from the discarded textiles of other family members, to link the baby to its kin and protect them using the strength imbued in these cloth pieces. Embroidery has long been believed to provide protection using the power of symbolism, the strength of nature through the plant-based dyes used to colour the thread, and the placement of this mark-making onto the entry points of clothing—necklines, hems, and cuffs. The floral adornments and geometric patterns are now seen as mere decoration, but they were first employed to ward off evil and protect the wearer. So much of this power is a result of the strength provided by the former wearer or the hands that did the weaving, sewing, and embellishing. In Hawaiian tradition, the mother's hands constructing a quilt for her baby transfer her energy and protection into the fibres. The interlocking of the fibres themselves provide strength. This idea is behind much of the sacred power given to something like an Indian sari—the uncut, continuous piece of fabric providing a protective shield around the woman.

As a bagmaker, I created a number of fabric vessels made from favourite pieces of clothing or the cherished items of someone who had passed away. One was for the daughter of a young mother who'd died of cancer. The bag was made from an old leather jacket and a blouse that had been worn by the mother, and the idea that her essence was somehow entwined within the fibres of these textiles seems logical. How else to remain close to the person than to get close to the materials they wore? I had a friend who couldn't bring himself to shop at a second-hand store for this very reason—he didn't want to wear the clothing of a dead stranger for fear they remained within the very threads of an old cardigan or pair of jeans. I never asked him how he felt about organ donation.

I thought a lot about what we'd found in that box in the basement. I felt sad for the owner of the house and what seemed like an emptiness in his life that he had filled with stuff. I knew, from my dad, that he would have been a man with a good deal of money. He was well-known and respected in the oil and gas industry. But you never would have guessed this, based on how he lived. Over the course of those weeks sorting through the contents of his house, we found very little of value. When we eventually moved on to the detached garage, we discovered a neglected economy car. When I turned the key in the ignition, the dash lit up with warning lights. The furniture in the house looked like it had been his mother's, and it was mostly sturdy and practical, no frills. Based on the extreme clutter, the rotting food in the sink and fridge and the soiled bedding, it was obvious the man never entertained. There was barely room to get in the front door. This house was full of stuff, filled to the brim, filling what appeared to be a huge void in his life, a loneliness I felt deep in my bones. As much as we made light of the weird shit we found or joked about the disgusting nature of the job, there was a sadness in the house that we both felt, moving through those cluttered rooms.

With the art of Kintsugi, broken pottery is repaired using lacquer dusted with precious metals like gold, silver, and platinum to draw attention to the cracks and scars. Kintsugi dismisses perfection as an unrealistic goal, and instead highlights the beauty of healing. It embraces the repair, the imperfect, and the asymmetrical. Instead of throwing out the broken pottery, it's put back together without the need to conceal the cracks. It's about resisting the urge to discard the damaged.

In recent years, the internet has churned out countless articles, Instagram posts, and inspirational quotes using Kintsugi as a metaphor for growing from failure and surviving through times of difficulty and loss. People are using the principles of Kintsugi on their own bodies, getting tattooed after mastectomies, owning and highlighting the beautiful scars of survival and resilience. It's interesting to me that people mostly want to hide their scars, that the body's strength and ability to repair itself is seen as something to be concealed. I've had numerous abdominal surgeries, including three C-sections, and one of the first items addressed by the physician in the pre-surgery discussion was the minimalization of the scars. I doubt the doctors think this important, but instead mention it because it's a priority for so many patients. When you have surgery, you've gone through something major. My scars, like photographs, are what's left behind after an experience in my life. They're triggers of memory, reminders of great joy, trauma, triumph, and resilience. They're tallies of my body's immense abilities, golden lines of repair on the vessel that holds me.

Later that summer, after the job at the hoarder's house was done, I went to a Pearl Jam concert with D and his girlfriend. It was general admission, and we waited in line from early that morning, hoping to secure a spot close to the stage. It paid off, and we ended up in the front row, right below Eddie Vedder's microphone. After the band had gotten good and sweaty playing songs like "Daughter" and "Rearviewmirror," a roadie threw them towels and Stone Gossard wrapped one around his long hair, like he'd just stepped out of the shower. He played the next song wearing the towel, then threw it into the crowd. I still have it today.

One of the last tasks we completed in the dead man's house that summer was opening the Christmas presents that were stacked beside piles of garbage. The wrapping paper was yellowed, suggesting the gifts had been received many years prior. In one box was a cordless phone, likely from a friend or family member who wished to keep in touch, to stay connected through the chaos of this man's home. I snuck it into my backpack. I didn't tell D. I knew he'd disapprove. We'd both been completely on the up-and-up about everything we found in the house, sorting it for donation and putting the items of greater value together for an estate sale. But I wanted this phone. I still lived with my parents, but I felt I needed it more than any thrift store. Two months later, I would be moving into that first, crappy apartment with the cigarette-burned carpet, drunk and high all the time, no longer welcome in my parents' home. That phone would keep me connected through the chaos.

On Identity

JAMES GOUDIE

Under the Influence

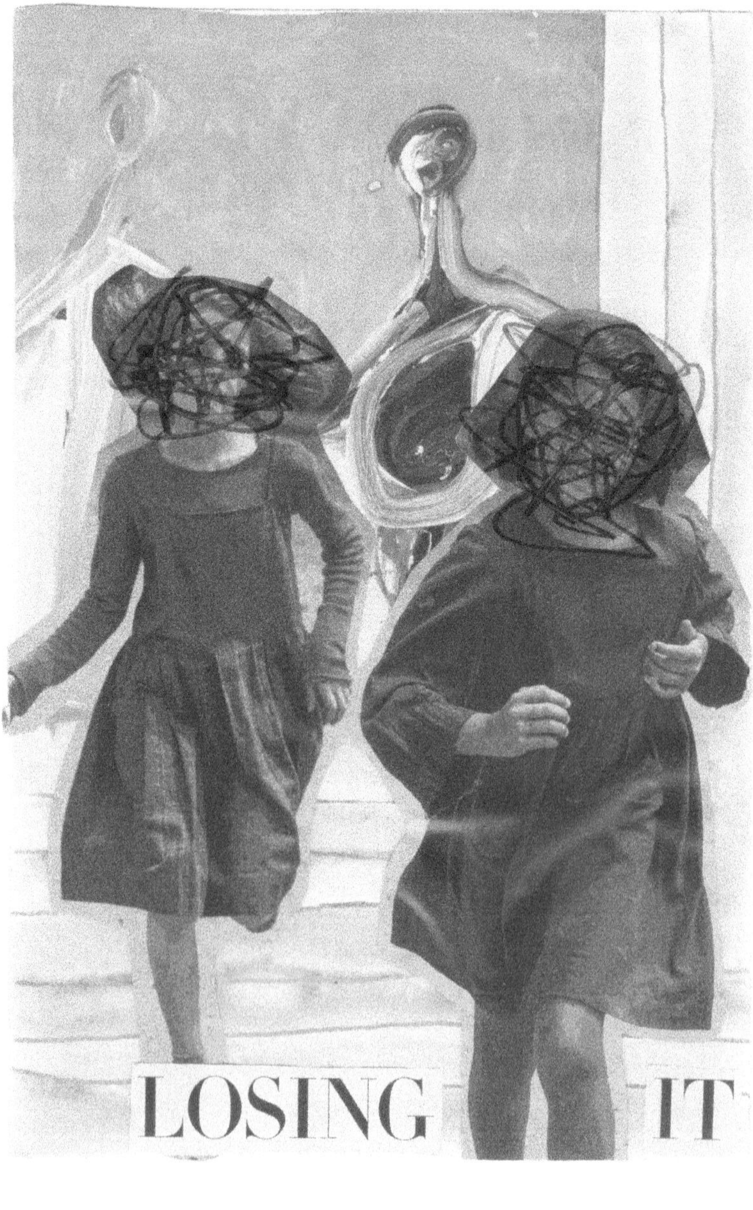
LOSING
IT

JAMES GOUDIE

Dinner with Enya

JASMINE BASUEL

Netty was kissed outside the apartment building. Her girlfriend's lips were dry and the press was quick and after she pulled back, Netty licked her lips like there was something to taste. A gust of happy air swept through her before the familiar girl who kissed her said,

"I understand now. Why you think we can't go on a trip."

Netty looked up at the apartment building. Four stories up she felt her parents cleaning the dishes in motions so practiced they never even thought to use the dishwasher. The kitchen cabinets slumped against bare walls wearing wallpaper peeling away from fifty-year-old glue. The vase of pert yellow flowers placed on the table before dinner. What was an indulgent vacation in the face of all that? How could money spent on a nameless island compare to money spent up there?

"I never said we couldn't go." Netty's voice came out soft. She kind of meant it.

Her girlfriend shrugged. "You might as well have. I mean. It would have been great to get away but now—"

"Yeah, I know." An aborted kick at the sidewalk. Guilt and pride wrestling.

"But now I get it. You can't go because of the whole money thing."

"What money thing?" Netty choked out. Pride, victorious.

Her girlfriend's forehead folded in on itself and she stepped back to look at Netty. "The money thing."

"There's no money thing." Netty's ears were pink. There wasn't a money thing. At least not a money thing that her girlfriend should know about. Nothing she could even understand. Not with her manicured nails and designer handbag and white parents and their acres-deep lawn. This was a gap she could never breach; a gap Netty did not wish her to breach.

The sun was branding itself on the last minutes of the day. The girl looked orange, swaying like a pale candle flame. Her hair was yellow. Netty almost forgot to be upset, she was so taken.

"Yeah, but it seems like there's a money thing. With your parents. And like. I get it. Immigrant stuff, right? I get it." Her girlfriend's confusion gave way to a satisfied kind of confidence, like she had solved something between them. Her body sunk into the feeling while Netty's spun up into her shoulders.

Netty frowned. "I seriously don't get what you mean."

"And of course there's all the other things with traveling. Like buying bikinis or like maybe just swimsuits if you'd like. And the food and transport. All those kinds of things."

"Is this about my parents?" *Am I now a stranger to you now that you know them?*

Netty's girlfriend gave a short laugh, confusion crawling up her back again, pulling tight across her green eyes. Even in sensing Netty's cooling, she was still so beautiful with her slender figure and straight nose. This girl was someone Netty had only dreamed about; something she had never allowed herself before. The girl replied, defensive, red cheeks against blue eyes, "No. Not at all. Why would you think that? I'm not like that."

Netty rolled her shoulders. Her coarse black hair barely scratched them. She felt the kitchen blending into the dining table with the plastic-covered chair cushions, into the plastic-covered couch and the ten-year-old television in the thirty-year-old cabinet and the browning doily on the coffee table. She thought about her two parents four stories up, saving the food from the plate the girl hadn't touched while the other plates were scraped clean. The plastic Christmas tree with a paper lantern shaped like a star on top. The pile of shoes at the entrance. The cross with a porcelain Jesus above the bedroom door.

"Did you like dinner?" This was all Netty could say. There was nothing else.

The girl's body relaxed. "I've never had food like that before. I liked it. Please let your mom know."

"My dad made it."

"It was great."

Netty licked her lips again and they started walking home.

Dermatillomania

AUTUMN H. THOMAS

Phone camera illuminating skin
                        reflection rocking back on its haunches
tv static engulfing, furrowing its way
inside my mind
                    You, or rather   the pixels of you
                    Tell me
                    Tell me
                    Tell me
                    Pixels of you.
                                        Its never too young to start retinol!

Check out which celebrity just started Ozempic! Check out this new drunk elephant
                    Product   *tik tok shop $2 off*   *we*
                                                Can't say whether these
                                                         Young girls
Should be using retinol   *but*   *our* product *is for* ALL AGES.

L
 i
       s   k e   curling his tail round my throat
   k   A   n a   *skin picking seems*
e   *to be an emotional*
                                                                                        pacifier

                When I lost my pacifier
                I buried it in the yard
                When I lost my pacifier
                When I lost my pacifier
                I buried it.

When I first wrote about it I made it a tango.
          Tango: *noun. A ballroom dance from*

                    verb: A code word for an enemy.

                                        i vomit the idea from the center of my
                                                                          mind

Try this foundation to make your skin
flawless.   *Trust me girls,*
                               I wouldnt have had a
                               chance with this star if it werent for

    Im picking my skin
a g a i n . again   I pick at my scabs   the spot behind my ear
                                              my forehead   the one in my
brain
I pick at it until it bleeds
puss filled pockets
So satisfying
I pick at it until it bleeds
like relief of abscess in
her old hoof, shes
Lame no more   *you know…*   *you really shouldn't have*
                                          Gotten yourself into that situation.

Just *relief.*

Dead Deer, Nebraska

GRAEME GUTTMANN

Two pumps stood against the land, the concrete, relics of the past. I wasn't sure they'd even dispense gas, but somehow I still had faith that things did what they were supposed to do.

I'd been driving faster than normal, but I slowed down when I got to Nebraska. There was so much land in front of me, it didn't feel like speed was making a difference.

I could feel a cavity growing in one of my left molars—all I'd eaten was stale candy from convenience stores that only saw a dozen customers a year—just enough to stay alive.

Some stores had other ways of making money—the pumps I pulled up to came with a man fishing something out of cooler. He turned to me; clear plastic bags filled with a deep red that could only be a dead thing. His liver-spotted hands shook as he held the meat, offered it to me.

what do you do with the rest of it—the guts and the antlers?

The deer man paused, considering whether my curiosity was the real thing.

most of the time it just gets thrown away. got no use for leftovers here. can't have dead things just sitting around.

I watched him walk back to the cooler, saw piles of red bags behind the stained silver door. He could put me in there if he wanted to. No one's looking for me. He could probably even sell me—*this one died young but sometimes that makes them taste better—*

Going home the weekend the boy I used to love died

GRAEME GUTTMANN

1.

I always arrive with a wound,
something for my mom to tend
to. She cuts my hair this time,
tells me he died the day before,
points out the deer in the yard,
tells me I need to take better care
of myself. I lock eyes with the stag
through the window until my gaze
scares it away.

2.

I cry while reading the news. He went right through
the windshield. Died on impact. He never
liked wearing a seatbelt or the way it wrinkled
his clothes. It would get in the way when we snuck
to his car during lunch, left campus to share cigarettes—
I was obsessed with the way his lips held the filter.

He was always careful with me—in the way his fingers
brushed my chapped lips, in the way his hands never forced,
only suggested. In the way he always had an excuse
at the ready in case we were seen together. We were always

partners for a class project, but I wanted to be caught in a position
where the lie would be clear like glass. Even the last time I saw him
when we were both in college, he winked at me while smacking
his gum, pulled me into a bathroom stall, left me there, the door ajar.

3.

I'm in the car with my father when we see the deer in the road,
neck split open. I think of him as we pull over, headlights
illuminating the animal's body the way only the dark allowed.
My dad took the buck by its antlers, dragged it into the grass, checked
to see if it was still breathing with two fingers on the bloodied neck.
I wondered if you can even feel a deer's pulse that way.

Can't Go Home

CHLOE TATE

Take me home, roots Home's
out- grew old a soda-
stained

map
mark I won't
drive
through
any- more

The Imaginers
ANTHONY CORREALE

In the Bubble, fertility accorded Ell a position of respect. She had been named Summer Clearance Event Debutante two years running, a red slash across her chest declaring "Everything Must Go!" The title landed her a coveted appointment tending The Mall as a Bath and Body Works Clerk. Mornings and evenings of each day, citizens would be allowed to enter The Mall and stroll its wide avenues perusing the shops, free to choose where they would pray. Ell met them at the front of the store and welcomed them with a "How may I help you?" repeated so many times that it acquired the maddening musicality of a jingle, the meaninglessness of a benediction.

In the early years, samples would have been given, dabs of perfumed soap and lotions, and the shoppers would be led through the expression of their wants. They would collectively imagine their homes, a bounty of plush towels in lilac and dove-gray, light and open to the wind, curtains billowing, letting in the sweet scents of Jasmine or Mango Champagne.

But by the time of Ell's Clerkhood, the supplies had dwindled. Many of the products had hardened or separated, breaking down, reverse engineering their synthesis and becoming again their foul-smelling constituent parts, the disembodied phonemes of a dead language, the coiled polymers of human ingenuity unkinking. They had lost the art of Foaming Exfoliating Action, Microbrasion, Anti-Aging, Volumizing Silk Proteins. Only the candles remained intact, so Ell would lead her shoppers between them so that they could engage in the imagining together—this was a "Crisp Autumn Morning," this was "Salted Caramel Chococcino." They passed the candles around and envisioned the places that belonged with the smells, the impossible reds and yellows on their labels a guide, an almost incomprehensible plenty of color. Each shopper would be allowed to light a single candle, watch the wax soften and the scent warm, and when there was enough to dip their finger in, they would daub themselves with a bit of that lost world—a single drop of "Winter Sunlight" or "Seafoam and Cedar" or "Margaritaville" on their forehead to armor their hope.

Swaying, their eyes squeezed shut with the force of imagining, Ell studied them skeptically. What was "Lemon Orchard Dew" to this man, really? Most of the shoppers were older than Ell, but they remembered even less than she did. They had been early admits, the children of shareholders given over for safekeeping. Their parents had thought they'd follow, but everything had happened too quickly, and the Bubbles had been put on lockdown when the program was still in trials. The promotional materials, still prominently displayed on the walls of each bungalow, declared the Bubbles "Humanity's Great Hope." Stocked, they claimed, with "The seeds of tomorrow!" The shareholders, though, had jockeyed for all of the slots, and nepotism had filled the rest. After all of the bribes and falsified medical documents, this Bubble—maybe all of the Bubbles—had locked down with a fertility rate barely better than the global average.

Ell had long grown sick of the Bath and Body Works, the glitter that never washed off, the smells coagulated into a single stench, like someone had tried to put out a plastic fire with vanilla extract. Ell had never found the imagining comforting. Unlike the imaginers, she hadn't chosen the Bubble. The others called her a late admit. Kidnapped, she corrected silently. Now, staring out toward the food court at where the Orange Julius stood empty, she knew she needed to get out.

"What is this about the smell? You should take that up with HR. Why haven't you coupled yet? You are putting the long-term viability of this venture at risk." The Chief Executives were displeased. They hemmed and hawed, fingered the gold tie clips bearing their titles in blue enamel, leather squeaking as they shifted in their seats. Yes, they agreed, you are free to make your own decisions. No, you have not violated the Corporate Code of Ethics. But. "Perhaps," said the COO, who had owned a ranch in the last years and looked at her the way he might have once looked at an uncooperative heifer, "we need to rebalance the incentive structure?"

Ell was in her mid-twenties—she couldn't be exact—and she saw that they would not allow her to remain uncoupled for much longer. Recently, words like freedom and choice had acquired a nasty ring.

Ell had coupled, though. Unauthorized. He was gone now, and if it was discovered that she had coupled with him, she'd be quarantined. Probably incinerated.

It had been the guy who tended the PacSun, in his pookah shell necklace and polarized wraparounds and torn boardshort vestments. Every day on her way to the Bath and Body Works, she passed him practicing his hacky sack routine in front of the Orange Julius. "Hang ten," he would say. She thought he might be winking behind his sunglasses. She was not interested. He was a regular at the Bath and Body Works, stealing in for a quick imagining on his fifteens. He would sit cross-legged in the aisle with a candle pressed between his flat palms, face a caricature of profound serenity. His candle: "Zen and Wet Stone."

Always, he prayed alone. Ell couldn't tell if it was by choice. The other shoppers were skittish around him because he was the nephew of someone who had been discontinued. A rare enough event, but this was an exceptional case: his uncle had been the CTO.

The PacSun guy persisted. He appeared for his imaginings shirtless, strutting down the aisles. In spite of herself, her eyes followed the ripple of his abdominals, gleaming from a liberal and not-recommended application of expired suntan oil. "How may I help you?" she asked him, perturbed. He'd been rooting through the loofahs, soiling them with his greasy fingers.

"I know you don't belong here," he said. "I can tell. I don't belong here either." He had leaned toward her conspiratorially, but now, pleased with himself, he struck a pose. She recognized it from the PacSun displays—a bare-chested man with a surfboard under one arm surveying the surf and the swimmers frolicking there, cocksure, mouth just slightly open. The imitation was good, but his sex appeal was limited by the reek of spoiled coconut. Ell ignored him and retreated deeper into the Bath and Body Works.

"Hey," he'd called after her. "Call me KJ!"

Ell should have expected that the Chief Executives would rebuke her. After she lodged her complaint, they reassigned her to the nursery. "We apologize," said the COO, officiously tapping the brim of his Stetson, "for having promoted you to the level of your incompetence."

They said: we think this position will allow you more time for personal development. They said: the matter is now closed and all further inquiry should be routed through HR. They said: be sure to wear your Debutante sash.

The nursery was a squat bubble within the Bubble, the epicenter from which the bungalows and Champotater beds radiated outward. To enter, Ell had to pass through an extra-precautionary decon cycle like those that the incinerator crews who regularly suited up and ventured out to burn the jungle back did: bite into the oxygenated mouth-piece, close her eyes while blue-white powder sifted across her body, was vacuumed, sifted again, vacuumed, and finally a steam cycle. An acrid taste lingered on her lips and when she absentmindedly licked them, her tongue went numb.

The inside of the nursery was optimistically vast. Eerily empty with only five children in residence. One side of the structure was dedicated to the birthing rooms, but they were locked up now. Five years had passed since a birthing room was last used and there were no current pregnancies. Despite their mandated hours in the skylight room, the children were pale enough to recede into the milky walls. All of the citizens were a little pale, the Bubble screening them from much of the sunlight, but the children, who would not leave the nursery until after puberty, were flittering phantoms. One looked particularly sickly.

"Weak heart," a man confided. "He'll probably die soon." He was stroking his long tie—red to denote viable sperm count. Ell turned to look at him, and he unfurled a wide, sharky smile. The nursery was a cautionary tale. This, the Chief Executives were telling her, was why she needed to couple. Here, wearing a boxy suit and hair so shiny he must have lacquered it with product after completing the decon, was how. She supposed this was their attempt to reason with her and she was free insofar as she chose to interpret the warning.

After coaxing the children to breakfast on their bowl of pureed Champs, they showed instructional cartoons on a screen hooked up to an old DVD player. The schedule posted to the wall mandated they show the cardinal rules after breakfast and before bedtime. There was "Stay Out of Trouble, Stay In the Bubble!" and "Boil Before You Drink!" and "Watch and Report!" The last was the longest, displaying a series of known threats and their identifying markers: this was a slipworm larva, these were the early symptoms of a silverpin infection. Ell had never experienced those, but she tensed when the segment on Jasper Beetles ran: a little boy extends his hand to a beetle and gently spoons it a single drop of porridge. The beetle trembles a moment and then, with a *pop!* multiplies into a swarm. The frame zooms out and *pop!* the swarm doubles, filling the entire bubble. The mass of beetles pulses, straining, and then *pop!* blows through the bubble, dispersing and leaving nothing but shuddering skeletons and empty frames that sway a moment before collapsing onto the scraped-clean earth.

Her family was one of the first to leave in the Flight, so early that it was not even called that yet. So early that they were considered kooks. Her father, with his minor leagues cult charisma and his trailing prophet's beard had stood atop the roof of their Subaru Outback, immovable in their driveway for want of fuel, and declared that he was leading his people into a northern wilderness untainted by the evils of civilization. The other families, gathered in their suburban cul-de-sac to hear him, shuffled uncomfortably and shook their heads. The next morning, though, as Ell and her parents shouldered their packs, a handful of other families appeared, and they set off as a caravan. Her father led, making up pilgrim hymns as they trekked.

Ell was ten—the last age that she could remember marking, the last age she could be sure of. The Corporate calendar was so different, omitting seasons in favor of Mallidays and smoothing the years into a blur, that she did not even know her birthday anymore. That long journey north was difficult for her to recall, the transition between one life and another, undefined by any logic that she could discern. Weeks of walking, the adults thinning beside her, faces roughening. What she remembered instead was listening for the sound of the Jasper Beetles' approach. They were an elemental force, forming tidal waves that crashed across the land, so tightly packed that the friction of their chitinous bodies presaged their arrival, a grinding roar. The swarm was the weather they feared most, the distant rumble enough to send them scrambling for shelter.

She remembered walking onto a farm somewhere in the middle of what had been Minnesota, scorched-looking after the swarm had mowed over it. The farmer had been left beside his ruined crop. She'd seen plenty of dead bodies by then, and she'd thought, at first, that he had begun to bloat. But his corpse had been heavy with beetles, and as she approached, she saw them spilling from his mouth like slithering jewels, topaz and tiger-eye.

Her mother told her that the beetles' nerve columns were gnarled into fists that no poison could unclench. Humanity, her father added in his sermonizing voice, had been so self-involved, so small-picture, that it had initiated a biological arms race that it could not possibly win, and when it hesitated, when it teetered—just an instant—it had fallen impossibly behind and been swallowed. Another of the adults crossed her arms and muttered something about vaccines, a third rolled his eyes and the assembled group was off, barking at each other and stamping their feet.

They were prone to arguing about these things, the source of civilization's ruin. Sabotage. Hubris. Sin. Microwaves. Only Ell's mother did not participate in these debates. "Utopia has to figure out its original sin before it knows what it's built around," she told Ell once. She was cracking sticks and arranging them for a fire while Ell's father polemicized. "But they haven't realized yet that we're not utopians."

"What are we?" Ell had asked. But her mother hadn't answered. All of them had quieted and were watching the evening sky. The horizon popcorned with exploding satellites, countless of them, their fragments streaking to earth.

Sometimes the adults told the children in the nursery scary stories. It was rumored that one of the other Bubbles, Conagra maybe, or Unilever, had collapsed after a slipworm outbreak. The CEO's wife had been pregnant, and when she gave birth they had realized that the child was too still, but they were hopeful: it seemed to be trying to open its eyes. Looking more closely, though, they saw that it was only a boil of worms writhing behind the closed lids. The worms had somehow infiltrated their water supply and spread into most of the population (*Boil before you drink!* the children chanted) before they were caught. They tried to quarantine, to burn it out, but within a week, everyone in the Bubble was sterile. After that? The children asked, What happened to the people? But no one knew. Ell liked to imagine them simply opening the doors of their Bubble, letting the outside air in. They would tie their dresses and suit pants around their heads and scamper into the jungle in their underwear. If there was nothing to hope for anymore, what was there to fear?

When they were not being instructed, or cajoled to eat their Champs, the children played games. They'd choose a victim, usually the sickly boy, and they'd dance in circles around them, chanting the names of the plagues—Rotslick, Medusa Liana, silverpins, slipworms—and they'd wriggle their fingers all over the victim, whose job it was to kneel and display the symptoms: vomiting, lung-dredging coughs, seizures. The sickly boy did not like playing, did not want to act as though he was wasting away from Rotslick, or stagger drunkenly as though silverpins had penetrated his brain, but they forced him. It was their favorite thing to do and they could play for hours, departing from the known threats and imagining their own horrible recombinations and monstrosities. When the adults wanted them quiet, they gave the children charcoal and paper and they sketched their monstrosities. The walls of the nursery were papered with wasted grayscale landscapes of insectile giants and writhing boils and grotesque things for which only the children had names.

The minders sat idle at the periphery while the children entertained themselves. Everyone studiously avoided looking at Ell, leaving her to the attentions of the sharky man who insisted on wearing his power tie and shellacking his hair every day. He tried to make small talk while the others flipped through the official circulars that the Chief Executives released weekly. Their headlines declared atmospheric scrubbing underway, experiments with resistant corn seeds promising, yields increasing. In too-loud voices, the minders spoke about them to each other while the man went on schmoozing Ell.

"The Polar Realignment should be near finished. Then it's only a matter of time—maybe three or four years—and things will be back to normal."

"Yes, partnering with Boeing too. They know what they're doing."

The sharky man cleared his throat. "So," he said sporting his toothiest smile, "are you ovulating?"

"There's been a quarterly uptick in fertility rates," they were shouting. "Teste parasites are at a five-year low." Just then, the sickly boy broke down, wailing, and Ell rushed over to stop the game. The man stayed behind, smoothing his long red tie impatiently. According to her chart she should be ovulating, but she wasn't. She'd been off the chart completely for weeks.

The next time that she had seen KJ, he'd motioned to her from the Orange Julius's kitchen as she walked past. "I have something to show you," he said.

She shook her head. "I'm not going in there with you."

He looked pained, but he tip-toed out into The Mall's wide corridor anyway, a sheaf of circulars in his hand.

"I found these in my uncle's things," he stage-whispered. "Check it out."

Ell didn't recognize the headlines. What he was showing her, she realized, were intended to be the last circulars, the run that had announced the dissolution of the Corporate Bubbles. The language was cheery. There were even sidebars with motivational quotes: "Failure is the mother of invention!" and "If at first you don't succeed, try, try again!"

The Chief Executives had never distributed them, he said excitedly, choosing to wipe all of the dates and rerun the circulars starting from the beginning. "They've been lying to us all along!" he said. "There's no venture. The corporate charter is void. We're just prisoners. Who knows what's really out there!"

Ell studied him, the eager, open face. He was a little dumb, she thought sadly. That the Bubble had long since lost contact with the outside was no secret. The recycled headlines—they all recognized them. Everyone was pretending. Still, she stepped into the kitchen with him and leafed through the circulars. The Orange Julius somehow still exuded a faint scent, uncorrupted by the years, that she identified as "Dreamsicle."

"My uncle," KJ said, "he thought we gave up too easy. He thought we could harness it—the plagues. Make them work for us. We were focused on hiding, on cleaning up, but he thought we needed to embrace it. After we lost contact, he wanted to open the Bubble up." A rare cloud passed over his features, not brooding exactly, but not quite pouting. "I wanted him to take me with him, but he said I was too young and naive. He promised he'd come back for me." KJ grasped her hands in both of his. "I have a stack of CEO Gold Cards hidden away. I can get us out." She nodded along encouragingly. Because she did not belong; because she had thought many times of escape. And here was an accomplice.

"Wow," she said. He grinned and shrugged modestly, bouncing the hacky sack from one shoulder to the other.

"You've been out there," KJ said to her, "you must know. There's something. Right? A safe place?"

Yes, she'd said, thinking of the cabin her mother had built, the community they'd founded in the wilds but never managed to name. Never mind that she'd last seen it aflame—if she escaped, she could push even farther north, to the boreal forests. There had to be other isolated places.

They began meeting at the Orange Julius in secret after The Mall had closed for the day, fantasizing and planning for their escape. She came to understand that he believed the world he imagined in the aisle of the Bath and Body Works was still out there just waiting to be reclaimed. He *was* naive. But who was she to interrupt his imagining? It was there, on the tiled floor, beside the gleaming industrial-sized dishwasher, with Dreamsicle perfuming their nostrils and the hope of their utopias quivering separate but unburst between them, that they coupled.

Biting back nausea as the children slurped up their Champs, slipping away to the nursery bathroom to stealthily vomit, Ell worried that soon she would begin to show. The standard-issue dresses clung, and there would be no hiding it. Assessing her, the sharky man would notice the swell of her stomach, and just like that she'd be reported— an unregistered coupling. On her way home, she'd hear an insistent hiss and the Recall team would be darting after on their sharp black Segways. They'd quickly extract the name of the father from her, and that would be that.

KJ had been stupid. According to her meticulous arrangements, they would sneak out at prearranged times using one of the Gold Cards, and stash pilfered supplies in staging areas within a mile or two of the Bubble: vacuum-sealed Champotaters, spare clothing, water purifiers. At his insistence, he snuck out alone, a gallantry she allowed. But he was ill-suited to the subterfuge. Returning inexplicably late after one foray, he startled an incinerator crew and they had torched him, as simple as that. The Recall team in their pop-eyed masks, the ventilators bulging over their mouths like raw, exposed organs, went to work: his quarters were searched, dismantled, burned out, all mention of his name erased from the manifests. Ell feared that they would find something that would lead them to her. She could not sleep through the night, palming the keycard she'd insisted KJ give her for safekeeping, listening hard, plotting the quickest route to the exit. As though she could outrun the black Segways.

In the weeks after, deviating from her cycle chart, Ell hoped fervently that she had just gone sterile, but pregnancy was an unavoidable possibility now. The Recall teams remained wary and this time there was no preparation, no meticulous plan. She dressed as sensibly as possible, but she'd been off of manual work for so long that her wardrobe only held an assortment of summer dresses, printed with flowers and the Corporate logo. She chose the longest—just past her knees—and her only pair of closed-toed shoes. She gathered what else she could—sealed bags of Champotaters and water, a change of clothes—into a sack and snuck out of her bungalow before dawn. She swiped through the unguarded triple gates, each sealing behind her with a kiss of suction, and she was out.

Even in the dawn coolness, the air assaulted her bodily: a dull slap of heat and then the humidity clenching her in a tight fist. She panicked—she had no physical memory of heat like this, of air so dense that it lumped in her throat and caused her to gasp wetly. She stood on a loading dock chewed at the edges by the encroaching jungle and scorched black from regular burnings. An umbilicus of asphalt, edges indiscernible beneath the crowding vegetation, twisted off. On the lip of the loading dock, she looked back at the Bubble. Craning her neck, she could barely see where the thick, moiré-patterned dome began to curve away. The jungle surrounding it was all untraceable knots and hooks trembling with malevolent intelligence and shot through with the hysterical chittering of alien life. Directed, it seemed to Ell, at the walls of the Bubble: the jeers of an invading force encircling the besieged.

To avoid brushing the feelers of jungle that strained towards each other over the once broad road, teeming with what she could not imagine, Ell had to fold tightly in on herself, sometimes turning sideways and awkwardly pliéing with her sack balanced atop her head. Her summer dress was wrinkled and sticky against her and she felt as though she were in a steam cooker. She feared the inevitable moment when the thin blade of cleared road vanished, the jungle knitted solid.

Instead, all at once, the jungle growth ceased without apparent reason, clearing the road and leaving the ground naked and fuming, the same sulfur-yellow as the sky. The soil seemed to breathe, damp and halitotic, and she instinctively brought the sweat-soaked collar of her dress up over her nose and mouth. She was approaching a T-intersection, this road even wider than that which led to the Bubble. Ell had seen maps in the papers KJ inherited from his uncle—all burned now—and knew that this was the ring road that circled the Bubbles. Through the bare streak of blight, she could see some of them littering the horizon, dull golf balls in the rough.

Though the rising sun was difficult to locate behind the petroleum smear of sky, she oriented herself to keep it on her right, approximating north. To her left, she saw the Spires, hazy in the distance. Taller than the Bubbles, bent over and spinning in an unnatural way that repulsed the eye, seeming to twist and break and lurch upright again. As the road circled the Bubbles, the Spires described another circle, a protective barrier. Though she thought she could detect something off with a couple of them, something off-kilter, and were those gaps in their line? She had no idea what lay beyond. Ell squatted in the road to rest, hypnotized by their motion.

She remembered passing them in the chopper. The sky had been black, stippled with funnel clouds, and as she watched, one of the Spires lassoed a nascent tornado and pulled it down, spinning impossibly fast, a filigree of lightning crackling around it. It had seemed to drink the tornado from the sky, and when it stopped spinning at last, the storm had calmed.

Ell hadn't truly known what to expect outside of the Bubble. She'd read the reports but she hadn't known what to believe after so many lies. She was startled to realize that somewhere deep she had secreted the hope that she would walk out into the neatly ordered world of her childhood, all squared off and smoothed over, the colors tamed, deliberate, like the houses and yards glimpsed on the candles' graphics. Her last impression of the outside had been from the belly of the chopper that took her to the Bubble, she the prize of their last search for late admits. The patchwork landscape below was emptied but still recognizable—silvery veins of highway supplying the branching fronds of suburban neighborhoods, occasionally even fields farmed recently enough that their herringbone patterns were still discernible. All of it there, if rapidly splintering at the edges. Still recoverable. She wished now that she knew how many years had passed. It didn't matter: enough that everything was unrecognizable.

The Corporate search team had found the community that her parents had formed, hidden in the cold temperate forests in the north. A virgin community, it was classified, because they'd managed to outstrip the most virulent of the plagues and their disastrous remedies and establish themselves in an ecologically isolated safe-haven. But the company men had landed en masse and herded them into the wide bellies of their choppers, and whisked them to a field hospital for decontamination and processing. Ell and a handful of other children were separated out from the adults and placed in a nursery much like the one in the Bubble.

After a week there, becoming accustomed to the papier-mâché texture and flavor of Champs and leading the other children through nursery rhymes adapted from her father's prayers, the corporate men had sealed them into hazmat suits and divided them, one into each of the choppers waiting to distribute them to the Bubbles. Discontinued, they had said, when she asked about her parents. Discontinued. She couldn't remember when she stopped having to ask what that meant, just that it had been after she realized she'd never see them again.

A few hours on Ell was flagging badly, everything swimming nauseatingly through the amniotic air. All of her imagining had failed to anticipate what had become of the outside, and she was beginning to panic. Several Bubbles were set close enough to the main road that their loading docks were visible, and she began to wonder if the keycard, still in her sack, would grant her entrance into their cool interior. Once, jogging by a Bubble, her flimsy flats already rotten in the humidity and flapping, an incinerator crew emerged. They wore slick black hazmat suits over their standard-issue polo shirts and summer dresses, Dow Chemical decaled in red. She wondered if their Chief Executives had run the last circulars or held onto them like hers, if they maintained the same blind hopes or if they had formed new ones. She wanted to ask, but she couldn't of course or she would die like KJ. The incinerator crews were on strict orders to burn anyone who approached them, even to burn any one of theirs that might be thinking of running. The jungle was nearly up to their loading dock, and as she trotted out of view, she heard a sound like the intake of breath as the flamethrowers started up.

Another Bubble had been impaled by a Spire. A storm must have uprooted it, hurled it like a javelin. The Bubble still stood, but it was fractured and jungle had already begun to scramble across it like a trellis, reaching all the way to the protruding Spire's end and hanging it with vines, like a pennant.

She guessed that it should be approaching noon, but the sky had soured, its yellow browning, and as she paused to try and track the shift, the whole canopy bowed heavily and began to fall. The first bit settled over her shoulder, kelp-like, wet and gluey and the same rotten avocado the sky had become. She'd peeled most of it off when a broad sheet landed on her bent head. She looked up, stupidly, and it adhered to her face, covering her eyes and nose and mouth, sealing her in and suffocating her with the smell of scorched rubber and plaque. How she wished for a huff of "Seafoam and Cedar" now. Or no, not that—the smell of snow. She would collect snow to melt for drinking water, and she loved nothing more than to rest her face in the bucket and breathe in the cold of it.

When the choppers had come, her father climbed atop a boulder and spread his arms in defiance, bellowing. He posed as though imagining himself illustrated alongside his words. Ell's mother gathered the children and herded them through the trees. They stumbled through the forest, slapped dizzy by wet branches, lungs aching from trying to swallow their breaths, for half a day before the Corporates captured them. As they were closing in, Ell's mother gathered the children. "Believe whatever they need you to," she said, her eyes on Ell. "Until you need to believe something else." Only later would Ell begin to think that it was in answer to her question.

She opened her mouth wide for air, but the gunk stretched without breaking. Only after clawing at it for a few panicked moments did she puncture the seal, and still it was in her eyes, burning them. Sheet after sheet parachuted slowly down. The road ahead of her and the jungle beside gradually lost their shape and color until everything was diffuse, dirty light like the first eyes must have seen.

She staggered forward, hand cupping her mouth, occasionally shaking the built-up goop from her head. The surface of the road was gummy and sucked at her feet. The sheets wrapped her legs, shortening her stride. If she fell, she would be buried. Soon she was stooped and shuffling under the increasing weight, the light dimmer and dimmer, drowning in ooze like some reverse evolution. Headlines lifted from the circulars carouseled madly through her brain—Biomass Carbon Sequestering! Stratospheric Scrubbing! Coke Makes Progress Partnering with Nestle to Deacidify the Gulf with CleanCloud!

Her throat was clotted and her breathing whistled. She fell to her knees, hands butterflying desperately over her mouth to keep it clear. The pressure increased, swaddling her.

"Hold still," a muffled voice instructed her, "get a large breath and hold still."

The goop was sliding off of her, light, almost the viscosity of water. She cleared her eyes and blinked. Her vision bleary, brain thin from the noxious fumes, she thought she saw the artificially bronzed and glistening stomach, the leather-thong flip-flops, an expression almost too goofy to be handsome, so oblivious it seemed invulnerable, before she made out the figure of a girl standing over her. The girl worked the handle of a gasoline pump, producing a fine mist that dissolved the slime into a sudsy mass of brown bubbles. She wore an emergency blanket foil-side-out, neck and arm holes cut into it, and on her back a massive plastic reservoir filled with the liquid.

The sky had nearly stopped falling, and once the girl had cleared to her satisfaction, she openly studied Ell, taking in the flower-print dress with its Corporate logo cheerfully reproduced at the center of each bouquet.

The girl pointed the nozzle at her. "You're a corpie cow," she said. Ell opened her mouth to speak and the girl clicked the trigger, spritzing her. "Swish and spit," she said.

Ell spat, coughed painfully. Her voice was reedy. "There are people out here?"

The girl snorted. "More or less."

"Where are your parents?"

The girl frowned at her. "I'm not a child. Those of us who grew up out here, the Soothsayer says we don't have much in the way of an endocrine system. But I'm OK. You should see the giants."

"Soothsayer?" Ell asked.

"Yes," the girl said, helping Ell to her feet. "He'll want to meet a corpie."

Ell, still woozy from the fumes and with one eye on the still-peeling sky, obediently followed as the girl took her to the edge of a city, its busted skyline all broken teeth. Picking across a field of rubble, the girl located a set of stairs that opened into a maze of tiled hallways, more stairs, up and down and up and up again until they arrived in a vast arcade, the high-ceiling above them inset with intact but scummed-over glass. Art had been exhibited on the walls, and Ell guessed that the building must have been a museum. The labels on the canvases were "Cypress Swamps" and "Redwood Forest," but the paintings themselves had been pentimentoed over by new landscapes, leafy blue molds and reefs of woody fungus. The room was filled with salvage: boxes of batteries, split and foaming, a cracked gumball machine, a pyramid of computer monitors—there was no logic that Ell could see. In the center, atop the washed-up carcass of some behemoth engine, ventricles and cavities agape, stood the Soothsayer, a staff of twisted metal planted beside him.

He wore a red knit cap and a red kerchief wound about his mouth and throat, the rest of his face obscured by sunglasses, their huge globed lenses fractured and glittery like compound eyes, a blue duffel bag at his feet. His head swiveled side to side, surveying them, and after a moment he raised his staff and pressed it against his throat. When he spoke, his voice was a distant tremolo, like the radio broadcasts her family had huddled in to hear every night as they trekked north, fainter and fainter until they were only lapping fizz.

"And so," he warbled, "you have emerged at last."

The girl, squatting on the chipped tile, raspberried in exasperation and held her face in her hands. The Soothsayer had fixed his gaze on Ell, in her tattered flower-print dress. An iridescent cloak of metallic orange shifted uneasily across his shoulders. He raised his eyebrows at Ell's shock-blank stare and the cloak flickered across a spectrum from burnt orange to a yellowy green and back with a sound like marbles clicking in a bag.

"What is it you want to know?" he asked Ell.

"I'm not sure," Ell said, glancing uncertainly at the girl and readjusting the sack, stalling, "I'm just following her." The Soothsayer spread his arms and the cloak began to crawl and chitter. Beetles, innumerable, draped in sheets across his body—Jasper Beetles Ell realized with panic. The Soothsayer swayed and ululated, the machine shearing the heights of his voice flat and dull, and the mass of insects rippled and vibrated, thousands of wing casings snicking open and closed.

"He's just showing off," the girl whispered. From her knapsack she withdrew a candy bar, still wrapped, liquid from the heat. With her eyes steady on the Soothsayer's, the girl tore the package, squirted a gooey jet into her mouth, and then tossed the remainder at his feet. In a mad boil, the beetles abandoned their formation and fell upon it, blotting it out. The Soothsayer stood naked, slicks of oily black formed concave sores across his chest and legs.

"Nasty child," he said. The sores wriggled with fat translucent larvae. Several plopped to the ground and he bent with startling agility to tweeze them gently from the ground and replace them in the nursery of his chest.

"Gross!" the girl declared, pointing.

The Soothsayer glowered at her. "Your ignorance is unbecoming."

The Soothsayer reached into his duffel bag and withdrew an assortment of junk—circuit boards and resistors, LEDs, the small bones of animals, the hollowed carapaces of insects, nuts and bolts—and rattled them in his huge cupped hands like dice. The beetles obediently rose and helixed around him.

"Now, seriously, ask me the question," the Soothsayer said. "I am attuned. I can give you the answers that you seek."

She clenched her dress—*silverpin, slipworm*. She squeezed her eyes and thought of the forest—how many miles? "No. Whatever it is, don't tell me," she said. But he resumed his ululations anyway, body jackhammering as the beetles twisted around him faster and faster.

He flung his hands wide, spilling their contents onto the floor, an incomprehensible jumble. Just as they were crescendoing, his wails were lost in hail of glitches and quarks.

Abruptly the Soothsayer stopped, the thrown bones and components forgotten. The beetles broke formation, forming agitated spicules that stabbed testily at the air. The girl stood as erect as an antenna, the gas pump's nozzle pointing upwards, turning slowly as though scanning the blank sky.

"Interference," she said. The Soothsayer was still, but his voice equipment squealed and clicked like a metal detector. "There's something coming."

"Yes," the Soothsayer agreed, voice steel wool on a washtub, "we are being stalked. A hoarder of knowledge, an amasser of keys. It is close on our heels, shod in darkness. It feeds on words, splits them like atoms and leaves a rippling slag of logorrhea in its wake. Knowledge melted incomprehensible. Glyph and symbol without interpreter. And when there is nothing left, we will be left to slowly die in a world that we cannot remember creating."

The beetles pulsed for a few moments, whingeing like a strained engine before returning to their host. The Soothsayer groaned and began to flail again, his voice tugged as though by some magnetic force into a theremin keening. With a final, desperate whine, the sound cut. His erratic movement shook his kerchief loose and it unwound, revealing a red power tie. A CTO's gold tie clip sprang loose and clinked into the recesses of the engine. Rotslick had consumed the lower portion of the

CTO's face, and as she watched, maggots began to froth out of what remained of his mouth.

She fled through the galleries, the canvases—"Great Plains" and "Florida Keys"—gleaming wetly with their brainless new growth. Past heaping bins of salvage, some of it looted from the Bubbles, down seized escalators. Deeper and deeper. This, she realized, had not been a museum but an airport. She found herself in the bowels of some long-dead transit system, running along the tunnel. Faint tissues of light settled on the edges of things and other people, child-sized like the girl, crabbed along beside her, their bodies whispering against each other. She heard the clink of a hammer, growing louder. A regular flash of sparks.

As she passed, Ell saw in the spark light a ring of blank-faced, child-sized people squatting silently around a man who, even kneeling, was as tall as she was. They watched intently as he hammered the track flat. The dull shine of beaten metal extended past them as far as she could see. If KJ had followed her out, he would have died a dozen times already on the way, but she longed still for his blind optimism. On the day he was incinerated, she'd been summoned outdoors by a contamination alarm. They'd all been in line, waiting to undergo an emergency decontamination. The Recall team had collected KJ's body and paraded it past the line in a clear plastic sheath, a warning. He hadn't even had time to wipe that idiot grin off of his face. It had burned there.

She emerged from the tunnels through a terminal of steel struts glittering with clinging glass, like the skeleton of a rolling wave. Overhead, the sky had been replaced by some awful kind of weather. It approached in jerks, an injured creature dragging itself. Something strained from behind it, a darker shape resolving. The enormity of the motion made her stomach twist, a little flip.

Ell unslung her sack and opened it. The vacuum-sealed plastic was torn and beetles tunneled merrily through the Champotaters. She withdrew one, antennae waggling from half a dozen holes, and bit into it. How many things did she already carry within her, she wondered, chitin crunching between her teeth, an acrid squirt of something peppery. She took another bite, considering the lurching sky.

Said the Lily Leaf to the Slug

KARAGIN RUFF

Once you break soil,
open your mouth
like a guillotine.
I welcome my beheading.
Guide me through
your radula and pharynx.
In your esophagus,
leave me lingering.
You loveless slug
who craves fresh salt,
come, kiss me, your lily leaf.
Let me satisfy your appetite.

One of These Things First

AMELIA K.

Ghost girls are easy to raise. They do not change shape like 2 liters of store brand cola left too long in the fridge, for nights when there is no water. They do not attract crumbs like a licked finger along a baseboard, for days when there is no food. Benign, docile, they neither burn nor blister in the sun; or the moon, for that matter.

The moon speaks simply, like a child, with all the patient frustration of a Monday morning quarterback. The moon wants liquid and hushed, like a new god, sweet and sly and approachable.

On the topic at hand, if you listen carefully enough: a ceaseless canticle of mothers say things like *Ghost girls are better off this way. Ghost girls are happier this way.* The mendacity!

Ghost girls could have been antibiotics. They could have been eraser shavings or treasured craquelure or beach towels or bugs squished accidentally, then purposely. A frostbitten nose, eaten during famine. A steering wheel, a stone in Tyro's pocket, a voice, a restful valley. The last $20 you ever owe. The vulture that ate the cat that ate the canary that ate the worm in your apple. A realized, rosy baby, in someone else's arms. Why not? The amount of matter in the world remains constant; this is known. Go out looking for ghost girls and you'll find one, sure as shit on your Sunday shoes.

Ghost girls move out of the hands of angels and into the hands of sorrow, who loves to drop them like eggs into batter, any batter, and mush and mush and mush them until her arm hurts. Good to the last drop, they are forgotten as quickly as they are eaten. They never make it to rot.

Of Course You Can't Really Change Anyone

WESTON CUTTER

Bowling league was Mondays, softball Wednesdays, so usually it was Thursday nights Dad'd take us three to the garage for shoe polishing. Probably only happened a dozen times, but I've asked Audra, and she remembers it being monolithic, something we Had To Do, like church or being extra nice to Mrs. Fisher. Bethany remembers the shoe polishing—she would've been 5, I was 10, Audra 8—but not as much Like A Thing, but she's the youngest and has lived in pained certainty she's always missed the juiciest part. Mom was around: I can't remember her but she had to have been there, infinite and ceaseless, otherwise we'd've been unwashed and frantic, the house lurching like broken polka toward disaster, and Dad would've screamed—about something stupid we'd done, about the lack of rain or too much rain ruining the grass, or the shitty drivers on his commute, or the Bjorklunds and their goddamn addition—till the shingles sloughed off and the siding fell away and the Capecchis across the street called the cops.

The shoe polishing was one of few doors Dad left open for us. We couldn't talk about monthly reports or efficiency tables, and when we dressed up he'd scoff at the ties I'd fasten to my neck, snort when the girls'd don dresses and clutch clipboards, pretending to be receptionists. We couldn't grow mustaches, didn't know how to bowl or play softball or why anyone would like Michelob; we were, we knew, *insufficient* to the task of adult attention. But when he'd polish shoes he'd soften; his voice even changed. *See that?* he'd ask after he'd done a particularly good job, *See how nice that looks?* and we'd congratulate him, or praise him, and he'd shrug and say, *Hey, even a blind squirrel.*

One year he had a truck. Why did a plant manager for a corrugated facility need a truck? Things happen to you as kids; you don't get to wave your arms and complain it doesn't make sense. It was the truck we all remember—I asked Bethany two nights ago, up with baby Jenny, fussy and refusing to latch. *Yeah, we'd sit on the tailgate, right? He'd set our feet right on his thigh?* I remember the tailgate but not where he'd set our feet. There'd be a Twins game on the AM/FM hung by its handle on a nail in the garage, because he'd grown up with a father who'd hung an AM/FM by its handle on a nail in the garage. Because of them, the same hangs in my garage, too.

Half a mile from our house, the Highway 62 bridge spanned the confluence of the Mississippi and Minnesota rivers—our town's name derived from the Dakota word for *meeting of the waters*. That summer, the bridge closed for repairs. Mom and Dad must've told us it was going to happen, but all I recall is the sudden shocking silence. This was the suburbs; it wasn't city loud, not bad by any stretch, but the constant low-grade thrum of the highway that led to the bridge was noticeable for its absence when it ceased. It felt miraculous.

What Dad liked was caring for things—the garden, Mom (as much as he could), *maintenance*. You wanted to see a happy guy? See him on Thanksgiving, switching out the 9-volts on all the smoke detectors, or how every three years he'd re-wax the wood floors, how equinox days, March and September, were when he'd switch the furnace filters. There was a whole system for making blueberry muffins, and, when we got older, he refused to allow any of us to leave the house without a few peanut butter and honey sandwiches packed for any drive or flight. We were terrified of him our first dozen years because it felt like living with a guard inside a museum in which enchanting displays loomed, or strange, small nooks of fascination beckoned, and each time we'd try to engage with any of it the guard'd rush over and scream that we were fucking everything up, that we should stop touching, would blow his top then walk away muttering, *It's not like what I care about's important! Who gives a shit what Dad wants!* Now we have kids and can sense how small he must've felt, unseen and desperate to roll some strikes, smash a ball, haul ass around the bases, slip through a few Michelob till things felt easier.

Audra remembers he did the shoes on rotation; Bethany can't

remember one way or another, and I thought he just did the same shoes, week after week. What felt essential was the inclusion—it wasn't grudging, wasn't cross. It also wasn't empathetic: he needed to polish his shoes, and the system he had in mind required us. "Hey kids, it's...*shoetime*," he'd say, flashing his hands—Jim Carrey's *The Mask* must've come out, and I sensed he was performing Being a Dad. It'd be after dinner, Thursdays, and I can't remember any weather one way or another from that year. Maybe the bridge closing and the road quieting made everything feel calmer and more enjoyable; maybe it was one of those magic Minnesota summers that rewards the suffering of its winters. We'd file out to the garage and he'd drop the gate of the truck and hoist Bethany up (but not me or Audra, which I'd find later broke her heart—Audra was only a pound heavier and 2 inches taller than Bethany, but she wasn't The Baby). We'd jostle for space and he'd come down the line, grabbing our feet, looking furious and exacting. *Hmmmmm*, he'd growl, and then he'd shove his size 12 Jos. A. Banks and Cole Haans and Florsheims onto our feet. The girls would squeal laughter and I'd smile and he'd crack the tiniest grin, like a felon getting away with it. He'd go quiet and drop to the task and sometimes we'd ask, and he'd tell us, again, how he built the shoeshine kit in his high school industrial arts class, and then he'd resume his quiet and listen to Herb Carneal's play-by-play and polish his shoes while we wore them.

We'd never wear them otherwise, and I don't remember the act feeling special, trying on Dad's stuff or anything. Mostly we were glad to be with Dad in a scenario that found him unlikely to get pissed.

We were supposed to be nice to Mrs. Fisher because her husband was dying, though he still wore a bathrobe to go get the morning paper at the end of the street, he walked fine, still smoked his pipe, still told us—if we happened to be playing basketball—the same old story of how he once made 31 free throws in a row at the YMCA as a young man. *Bullshit* we never said—old people were notorious—but you couldn't call old farts liars. So much of childhood is just fun things you're forbidden from, exciting things you can't say, and we weren't *bad* kids, but we wanted to know the edges, out beyond what we'd been allowed. Our dads were tired, overworked and stressed; our moms were kind and hesitant. That summer Mrs. Fisher asked us to weed her garden—me and Dan and Bob and Brian—offered us $2 each to do it. We figured it was because Mr. Fisher was dying, and as we talked about how we'd spend our money we made up stories—maybe she was in there having as much sex with him as he could since he'd croak soon and all we knew about sex was it was A Great Want. It must've been July. We went and, without speaking a word, pulled each plant from the earth—her tomatoes and spiky cucumber vines, her delicate little pepper plants and strawberries, even the Jack-in-the-pulpit, tucked over in the shade with its odd sensuousness. When Mrs. Fisher returned after twenty minutes, saying, *Let's take a look at your progress*, she clutched at her throat. All our parents gardened; we knew what weeds were. We knew what we were doing, and couldn't look at her when she paid us. The Fishers were unfailingly kind. Maybe that's all it was: we wanted someone to be reasonlessly cruel to. We spent the rest of the summer waiting for the punishment we knew would come when she told our moms.

Audra and I and occasionally Bethany would sneak out to Dad's truck some nights, sitting in the cab, snooping: had that package of Stim-U-Dent toothpicks always been there? That book of matches? That emery board? Was he having an affair, or did he have a drug problem? Our fears were established by sitcoms, our understanding of adulthood's challenges manufactured by TV. Aud and I agreed something was going on with Dad and we didn't understand. *Why's he so calm?* we'd whisper. It wasn't like Dad was skipping and whistling on his way in each night, but the house felt steadier. I wondered if Mrs. Fisher had told my parents about us ruining her garden, and I speculated maybe that's what he'd been waiting for—a little hellion rebel to relate to. I didn't know. Audra would tell me later she prayed Our Fathers each night that summer, as many as the date told her—she'd recite 5 on the 5th, 12 on the 12th. Ends of the month must've been brutal, and she thought maybe that's what'd caused the change.

Late that summer. I remember it was spaghetti night but perhaps that's just distance, longing. Not back in school yet, but we'd bought pencils and folders, there were lists—that interstitial anticipation. The Twins were bad, but we still polished shoes some Thursdays and listened to the games, watching our father's head bent to task. Maybe that's all he ever was trying to show: that there were Things You Should

Do no matter how you felt. You root root root for the home team even when they stank. You kiss your wife on returning from work even if you looked like you wanted to burn the world to ash, starting with your own life. You sigh like you've never been asked for such a great sacrifice each time one of your kids says, *Dad, can I tell you something?* but you say yes, and then stare at them, listening so intently they learn to keep it brief.

How's the Bjorklunds' new addition coming along? Mom asked, a soft arch to her voice. Audra and I stared at each other: *that's it*. With the bridge closed Dad must have had to take a new route to work, so no more driving past people he knew and felt competitive with, the parents of our friends and enemies from school. No more complaining about the Bjorklunds' gaudy addition (*They need another, what, 600 square feet?! Already live in a goddamn mansion!*), the Taurinskas' convertible, Janelle Scwarnick's new Mercedes now that she'd split from reliable Hank and had shacked up with that sleazeball surgeon Glen, the Garelicks' getting their goddamn pool redone. I was still looking at Audra, but not really: I was looking through her, wondering over little factors I'd never thought to notice.

He stood, neither suddenly nor loudly. He moved gentle, graceful, like I imagined he looked when bowling: all fluid. He was a pretty good man whose life sucked the stuffing and grace from him. He walked to my mother's chair, held out his hand, bowed just slightly and said, "Madam." We watched, forks quiet in our hands; we'd never seen anything like this, wouldn't ever again. For Dad's company parties they'd get gussied up and Dad'd nuzzle behind Mom's ear and she'd say, *Joshua Francis*, half scolding, half delighted as he asked one of us kids to take a picture of them, *An' try to get it in focus this time, wouldja*, and we knew something happened out there, wherever they went, or later, after they paid Samantha and he drove her home to return to a quiet house, but we couldn't see or understand it.

Mom tilted her head so minutely, like *huh, look at that*, then took his hand and stood beside him at the kitchen table and they danced slow together in a tight circle we weren't included in but recognized as where and what we must have come from. That tiny impossible distance between them and how hard they tried to cross to the other. I'd think of that moment two years later when I called him a fucking idiot—I hadn't really meant it, just wanted to see if I could get to him. He raised his arm and started to swing at me, and I thought *finally, do it*—maybe the whole time I just wanted to break him. He started fast—setting up for the kind of swat he took as a kid and told us about a few times—and slowed gradually and ended up gently setting the back of his hand soft against my cheek. *That'll teach ya*, he grumbled, and we stared at each other for a moment, both of us unsure how we'd got there, then never said another word, neither of us apologizing. Cynthia believes none of this: *Fuck you*, she'll say lovingly, teasingly, our daughters asleep upstairs, and I'll say, *No, it's true*, but I wouldn't believe it either. How could she understand the loving, generous man she adores was once a shadowy, bitten, wracked man, knocked around by such currents? After they rebuilt the bridge—it took a year, during which Dan and Bob and Brian and the rest of us neighborhood boys would sometimes bike out at dusk to its edge, as far as we could go, daring ourselves to look out and over the 70-foot drop—I don't remember Dad complaining anymore. I never thought to ask if he ever went back to his old route to work. I should ask. Maybe he still complained but finally learned to make it private, quieter. Maybe he simply needed a break—as we all must—from the slow steady accumulation of all he couldn't help becoming.

A Color of Wheat to the Forest Wall

L. WARD ABEL

Across the ragged field
        green at ground level
        but with distance
running a color of wheat
        to the forest
        wall—here barn fragments
and bones of long-gone farmers
        scatter across
        last year's planting.

The fence line
        remembers its cattle
and angled rocks
        their broken plows.
Timbering.
        Trash
along a crease of fallen leaves
        near columns
        planked
needing paint.

        I need paint.

I'm clapboard, plastic panes and
        gray lumber flapping.
I lean, I teeter, I dissipate

shack-torn by easy raining
        a bare hardwood edge
disheveled beside the parcel
        that's now a faded
        yardish
patch.
        Other wings
lose no departure
        in beautiful
        ruin.
My stay dulls
        into a later

        leaving.

if you had truly tasted the rainbow, you would know it tastes like the drive to Great Smoky Mountains National Park in the fall

MACK ROGERS

i am telling you, you have not witnessed beauty like the trees
        on 441 with nearly 18,000 acres ravaged by the wildfire
        as a backdrop.

it's like meeting a white boy on Grindr and driving to
        Cherokee from Morristown, TN to meet him
        every weekend.

the beauty of being introduced to other queers
        with a fuck-me smile and watching
        Drag Race for the first time.

it's driving to Cherokee to drive to Dollywood to walk around
        then back to Cherokee and back home and we're
        not even fucking anymore.

it's a beautiful day here and i am spending it
        with a boy unafraid of uttering hate who loves me
        because i am used to the scarcity.

it's the spark that's beautiful, of course,
    the thrill of love and the subsequent
    ghosting of it.

---

this is the world on fire and
    it tastes just like Dollywood
    Coca-Cola.

Coupon Royals

ARI KETZAL

If dollar-stretching were a sport, my mother deserves a place in the coaches' hall of fame. She'd take her crumpled dollars to the gym, by which I mean the grocery store, and she'd tell them, "Loosen up, y'all. You got dancing to do." They'd proceed to pop their joints, flex, and lengthen inside her cheetah-print purse while she steered a buggy with at least one squeaky wheel whining down the aisles.

Tales of coaches grow taller than the pines in Alabama. My mother and her dollars lived on the level of myth.

Every Sunday afternoon, my mother unfolded the newspaper and snatched out its heart: the coupon inserts. Mom pronounced them "Q-pawns," so I thought of coupons as a compound of Q-tips, for which the Q stood for "quality," and chess pawns—numerous, the humblest pieces in the game. We could win the game if we collected enough coupons. Differentiating what within the glossy pages was useful to our family from what was irrelevant felt like a treasure hunt. I was thrilled to be my mother's accomplice, armed with the adult scissors, clipping away at pictures and barcodes. We'd snip the worthy coupons out and slip them into a gallon-sized Ziploc bag she'd purchased with the aid of a coupon.

We didn't organize the coupons in binders like the coupon queens did, but my mother, in her own way, was coupon royalty, and royalty is passed down, so that meant I was, by blood, a coupon heir. We'd stand in line at the grocery store and I'd shuffle through the paper scraps in the coupon bag while she piled our purchases onto the conveyor belt. This was not an abnormal sight among people in the checkout line during the early 2000s. Since I left Alabama, I never see shoppers fumbling through their massive coupon collections at registers anymore.

Something else I rarely see anymore is the free catalogs that used to arrive in the mail addressed to my mother, who almost never bought anything from them. She simply liked to look. She'd celebrate the arrival of each catalog with a trill of delight. "Penney's is here!" my mother would say as if JCPenney had been a childhood friend who'd lived up the street. Usually the catalogs showed up within days of each other, so she'd have perusal material for a while after periods of catalog drought. She'd sit on the couch with a glass of Diet Coke and a catalog as thick as a phonebook, where, over the next several hours or several days, she'd carefully consider each photo of clothing, bedrooms, and kitchenware. My favorites were the slimmer L.L.Bean catalogs because I thought they were funny—how the people inside dressed plain but still expensive, and I, Southern as I am, was fascinated by the way the clothes tried to suggest a life of leisure and laid-back athleticism in some rocky coast/snowy forest world. The joys in browsing these imaginary lives: their textures, colors, patterns, and prices.

Catalogs are now more commonly digital, sparing trees and landfill space but leaving behind people with limited technological access like my mother. Mom's way with money taught me that one must often make sacrifices, and often one's decision won't satisfy all desires. That doesn't mean you don't aspire to fulfill those desires. You do more than try.

Once I attended a baby shower with people who, from what I learned about them, seemed to come from more financially and familially stable backgrounds than mine. When my friend, the mother-to-be, asked everyone to share one thing their parents did that was important in shaping the person they became, I talked about how, though my mother was always putting others' needs above her own—babysitting or substitute-teaching other peoples' kids in addition to raising her two—she loved yard sales. This was her ritual: on summer Saturdays, she'd wake before dawn, mark up the classifieds with her yellow highlighter, and plan out which direction to drive. She'd attempt to rouse me from bed even when

I declared I was sleeping until the morning cartoons came on. Yet I'd feel snubbed if she left without asking me. Now that I'm older, I'm as grateful for the days she left without asking as for the days she allowed me along.

Mom would drive to the subdivisions where wealthy people lived, the ones moneyed enough to place ads in the newspaper, and she'd stop at all the yard sales she spotted along the way. She wouldn't always go with the intent to buy. Sometimes she just wanted to see what other people were getting rid of, to imagine all the possible lives she could have with those objects, in those homes. Yard-saling gave her space away from my father, space away from her kids, a space all her own, and sometimes, when I was lucky, she'd invite me to share it with her. This is what I love about my mother above all else.

I told my pregnant friend to make space for herself in some way that brings her pleasure, and share that space sometimes with her child, but remember, foremost, that the space is hers.

Don't let your world take that away from you.

Mom made me feel we were outwitting a world that didn't want us in it. Outwitting, yes, the gerund, because survival demanded constant scheming with no opportunity for rest. Something that confused me as a child was how everyday speech in my mother tongue was embedded with the idea that there is shame in being poor and dignity in possessing wealth, even when the topic is no longer financial. "Poor" is a word also used to express pity, as in "you poor thing," or lack of quality, as in "poor soil," or sheer cruddiness, as in "poor grades." "Rich" is a word applied in situations of abundance: a "rich soup" may be intense or flavorful or fatty enough to be filling, while a "rich inner life" is a bountiful self-understanding or self-fulfillment. English's approach to these words helps fool people into believing that those with more money are more than those with less: more deserving, more intelligent, more healthy, more hard-working, more clean, more content, more virtuous, worthy of more respect. These ideas lead to people behaving in physical ways they may not even think about: talking down to restaurant workers, leaving messes for janitors, complaining about or ignoring people who have no housing, and so on. Ideas evolve into real incidences.

Coupons save imaginary money; because that money is never spent, it's not real. Money spent and money before it's spent is real. The catalog lives and the yard sale lives my mother imagined were real only to an extent, but my memories of my relationship with my mother that involve catalogs and yard sales are real. How can you keep in mind imaginary money so that your real money goes further? How can you coax a dollar to stretch?

Creativity. Creativity is the only way when one doesn't possess the tools others have. My mother's creativity, as with all forms of creativity, transcended financial value.

In algebra, the square root of a negative number cannot exist among real numbers, so to solve the equation, one must multiply a real number by the imaginary unit *i*. The solved problem will equal an imaginary number. The system of complex numbers is more inclusive than a system involving only real numbers. In the system of complex numbers, *i* can exist.

"You know I'm too cheap for that," I say sometimes to a friend who also grew up low-income and can hear what lurks beneath those words: that the value of my pleasure is not calculable in objects with price tags, the survival-pride in finding a deal when I do, a fear of what happens if tomorrow we wake up in a world too expensive for us. I'm cheap. Cheep, the sound of a joyful bird.

A week ago, an unexpected coupon for a free appetizer with the purchase of a specialty pizza from the local gourmet pizzeria arrived in my mail. What glee I experienced as I realized I could now afford this food from a restaurant normally beyond what I'm comfortable paying. I called someone I love who I wanted to share this meal with me. We made a pizza plan. Coupons are for tangible items, sure, but they are also for what life can be imagined with that item in it. There's nothing poor about that imagination—in fact, I'd call it not rich, but mighty abundant indeed.

Contributors

JASMINE BASUEL is currently pursuing their MFA in Creative Writing and teaching at Emerson College in Boston. They are mostly concerned with writing stories based on queer Asian American narratives. They have work upcoming in *Bodega*.

ANTHONY CORREALE is a writer from California and a lecturer at Clemson University. He holds an MFA in fiction from Indiana University and a PhD in creative writing from the University of Wisconsin, Milwaukee. His stories are forthcoming from *The Georgia Review* and have been published in *The Journal, Day One, Redivider,* and nominated for a Pushcart Prize.

WESTON CUTTER is from Minnesota and is the author of several books, most recently *Careful* from Finishing Line Press.

JANE FEINSOD is a poet and educator living in Philadelphia, PA. She received her MFA from UMass Amherst, where she was named a Rose Fellow. Her work has appeared or is forthcoming in *Redivider, phoebe, The Shore, Arkansas International,* and elsewhere.

CHAR GARDNER is a visual artist and a writer living in the Green Mountains of Vermont. For over thirty years she worked internationally as a producer of documentary films. Her essays have been published in *The Gettysburg Review, Green Mountains Review, Redivider,* and elsewhere. In 2013, she was the recipient of the Carol Houck Smith Award from the Bread Loaf Writers' Conference. Website for visual art: chargardner.com | Facebook: Char Gardner | Instagram: chargardner

JAMES GOUDIE is a Scottish-American artist currently getting a masters in Public Administration at Suffolk University in Boston. They work as a public servant for the Town of Belmont and volunteer for nonprofits in Massachusetts. Their undergraduate degree is from Syracuse University, where they studied Political Science and French/Francophone studies. Most importantly, James' lovely, overweight, 14-year-old cat is named Opie.

SOFIA GRADY shoots tequila, likes to dance, and perpetually has somewhere she should have been twenty minutes ago. She graduated from Emerson College with a Master of Fine Arts in Nonfiction Writing in the winter of 2023. In her work, Sofia strives for uncomfortable vulnerability—to place emotions on the page not often expressed, in hopes of inspiring audiences to do the same. Currently, she works as a fitness instructor in Boston, Massachusetts.

GRAEME GUTTMANN is an editor and writer based out of Boston, Massachusetts. He graduated with an MFA in Creative Writing from Emerson College in 2023. He works in entertainment media as an editor and film and television critic.

AMELIA K. lives in Georgia. She won Best of the Net (Nonfiction, 2024) and has appeared in *Dirt, Smashing Times, Hobart,* and others. Her chapbook *Amouroboros* (KERNPUNKT, 2024) was longlisted for the Kari Ann Flickinger Memorial Literary Prize. Her website is bio.site/ameliak.

ARI KETZAL grew up in several rural Alabama towns and currently lives in suburban Massachusetts. Awarded as a U.S. Presidential Scholar in the Arts for Writing under President Obama, their work has been Notable in *The Best American Essays* and a semifinalist for the Provincetown Fine Arts Work Center Fellowship in fiction. Their words have appeared in *Copper Nickel, DIAGRAM, Cream City Review,* and *Creative Nonfiction's* "Sunday Short Reads."

E.E. KING is an award-winning painter, performer, writer, and naturalist. She'll do anything that won't pay the bills, especially if it involves animals. Ray Bradbury called her stories, "marvelously inventive, wildly funny, and deeply thought-provoking." She's been published in over 100 magazines and anthologies. Her novels include *Dirk Quigby's Guide to the Afterlife:*

All you need to know to choose the right heaven. She's shown paintings at LACMA and painted murals worldwide. Check out her newest novel, *Gods & Monsters,* serialized weekly in print and on YouTube, and also available for listening on Spotify: metastellar.com/books/gods-and-monsters-by-e-e-king

HEIDI KLAASSEN is a Calgary-based writer and editor. Her work has appeared in *Salon, Redivider, The Saranac Review, The Calgary Herald, Westword, The Sprawl*, and more. Her collage essay, "Bicycle Trees" was nominated for both the Pushcart Prize and Best of the Net. Her personal essay, "Been Caught Stealing: Life Inside The Lorraine," was a finalist for the Digital Publishing Awards. Heidi is the executive director of the Creative Nonfiction Collective. She is currently pursuing a Master of Arts - Interdisciplinary Studies degree at Athabasca University, with a focus on literary and cultural studies.

MACK ROGERS is a queer Black writer whose work appears or is forthcoming in *Foglifter, The Offing, Glass, Shenandoah,* and elsewhere. Mack is a poetry reader for *Split Lip Magazine*, staff critic for Pencilhouse, and poetry editor for *Zero Readers Magazine*. His debut chapbook *Hindsight* is forthcoming with Diode Editions in spring 2025. Mack has been nominated for Best of the Net, Best New Poets, and the Pushcart Prize. He lives with his partner and their three cats in Raleigh, NC.

KARAGIN RUFF is a poet and fiction writer from Council Bluffs, Iowa. She graduated from DePaul University with a BA in English Creative Writing. Karagin Ruff is currently serving as an SCI AmeriCorps Fellow in East Boston.

ZACH SEMEL (he/him) is a poet and essayist with an MFA in Creative Writing from Northern Arizona University. Some of his previous work has appeared in *DIAGRAM, Salamander, The Brevity Blog, CutBank: All Accounts & Mixture, Drunk Monkeys, Flyway: Journal of Writing & Environment, The Nervous Breakdown, Wordgathering, FreezeRay Poetry,* and other places. His memoir manuscript was an Honorable Mention for Miami Book Fair's Emerging Writers Fellowship, and his chapbook *Let the tides take my body* was awarded the 2021 May Day Mountain Prize by *Hunger Mountain.*

CHLOE TATE is a Northwest Arkansas local whose work is indicative of intense self-discovery and a longing for absorbing the world's beauty. The queer artist has found solace in weaving larger than life worlds into their actual journey of healing and self-discovery, and strives to create space for others who have lost a connection to themselves and others. Their work is tying a string back to their core, with the hope others can also find use in their creations.

AUTUMN H. THOMAS is a graduate of Hollins University in the heart of the Blue Ridge Mountains of Virginia. She now lives in beautiful Prescott, Arizona continuing the art of observation while editing *Woodsqueer Literary Journal*. Her other work can be read in *Exist Otherwise, Active Muse, The Hunger, Belt Magazine, Children, Churches and Daddies,* and *Cleaver.*

L. WARD ABEL's work has appeared in hundreds of journals (*Rattle, Versal, The Reader, The Worcester Review, Riverbed Review, The Honest Ulsterman, The Main Street Rag,* others), including two recent nominations for a Pushcart Prize and Best of the Net, and he is the author of four full collections and ten chapbooks of poetry, including *American Bruise* (Parallel Press, 2012), *Little Town gods* (Folded Word Press, 2016), *A Jerusalem of Ponds* (erbacce-Press, 2016), and his latest collection, *Green Shoulders: New and Selected Poems 2003–2023* (Silver Bow, 2023). He is a retired lawyer and teacher of literature, and he composes and plays music (Abel and Rawls). Abel resides in rural Georgia.

KAMI WESTHOFF is the author of the story collection *The Criteria,* and the forthcoming *Sacral,* winner of the 2024 Floating Bridge Press Chapbook Contest, *Sleepwalker,* winner of the 2017 Minerva Rising Chapbook Contest, and two other chapbooks. Her prose and poetry have been published in various journals including *Booth, Carve, Fugue, Hippocampus Magazine, West Branch,* and *Waxwing.* She teaches creative writing at Western Washington University in Bellingham, WA.

Support Fork Apple Press

Fork Apple Press consists of three prongs — *The Core Review, The Juice Blog,* and *The Slice Contest* — that bite into themes and symbols of desire, consumption, spirituality, gender, environment, cultivation, and wildness. Each prong offers a different outlet, yet the fork forms a collective discourse circulating around shared topics. We seek to embrace each work's ability to introduce unique associations while standing in conversation with and juxtaposition against others. We're excited about pieces engaged with environmental justice, postcolonial feminism, queerness in all its humanizing and messy forms, and to support writers' expansion beyond these topics in ways that move them.

FORKAPPLEPRESS.ORG/ SUPPORT

Scan this QR code to learn more about ways to support Fork Apple Press.

FORKAPPLEPRESS.ORG/ NEWSLETTER

Scan this QR code to sign up for Fork Apple Press' monthly newsletter.